Praise for *A Field Guide to Happiness*

"Now, you've gone and done it, Linda Leaming. This book has impelled me to add a whole new country to my already-overflowing bucket list. But either way, I'm grateful for this most excellent field guide to happiness. Thank you, my fellow traveler, for sharing the love."

— Pam Grout, #1 *New York Times* best-selling author of *E-Squared* and *E-Cubed*

"Linda Leaming writes with a sweetness and an earned wisdom that goes down as smoothly as a good cup of tea. She is also very funny. If you are alive, or would like to be, read her *A Field Guide to Happiness* and find joy on every page."

— Eric Weiner, author of *The Geography of Bliss*

"Linda Leaming offers us a fresh perspective of embracing life's challenges while pursuing our dreams. Delivered with down-to-earth wisdom and intelligent humor, *A Field Guide to Happiness* takes us on a Himalayan journey to Bhutan while never veering far from the heart."

— Matteo Pistono, author of *Fearless in Tibet* and *In the Shadow of the Buddha*

"With Bhutan as a backdrop, Linda Leaming's intimate offering of life lessons in *A Field Guide to Happiness* encourages deep exploration in our own interior landscapes. This gem of a book is an invitation to know we have all we need to surrender in the arms of joy, and measure our aliveness with heartfelt connection instead of speed and productivity. Read it slowly and savor each morsel."

— Nancy Levin, best-selling author of *Jump . . . And Your Life Will Appear*

A FIELD GUIDE
to
HAPPINESS

ALSO BY LINDA LEAMING

Married to Bhutan: How One Woman Got Lost,
Said 'I Do', and Found Bliss

The above is available at your local bookstore,
or may be ordered by visiting:

Hay House UK: www.hayhouse.co.uk
Hay House USA: www.hayhouse.com®
Hay House Australia: www.hayhouse.com.au
Hay House South Africa: www.hayhouse.co.za
Hay House India: www.hayhouse.co.in

A FIELD GUIDE
to
HAPPINESS

*What I Learned in Bhutan about
Living, Loving and Waking Up*

Linda Leaming

HAY HOUSE

Carlsbad, California • New York City • London • Sydney
Johannesburg • Vancouver • Hong Kong • New Delhi

First published and distributed in the United Kingdom by:
Hay House UK Ltd, Astley House, 33 Notting Hill Gate, London W11 3JQ
Tel: +44 (0)20 3675 2450; Fax: +44 (0)20 3675 2451
www.hayhouse.co.uk

Published and distributed in the United States of America by:
Hay House Inc., PO Box 5100, Carlsbad, CA 92018-5100
Tel: (1) 760 431 7695 or (800) 654 5126
Fax: (1) 760 431 6948 or (800) 650 5115
www.hayhouse.com

Published and distributed in Australia by:
Hay House Australia Ltd, 18/36 Ralph St, Alexandria NSW 2015
Tel: (61) 2 9669 4299; Fax: (61) 2 9669 4144
www.hayhouse.com.au

Published and distributed in the Republic of South Africa by:
Hay House SA (Pty) Ltd, PO Box 990, Witkoppen 2068
Tel/Fax: (27) 11 467 8904
www.hayhouse.co.za

Published and distributed in India by:
Hay House Publishers India, Muskaan Complex, Plot No.3, B-2,
Vasant Kunj, New Delhi 110 070
Tel: (91) 11 4176 1620; Fax: (91) 11 4176 1630
www.hayhouse.co.in

Distributed in Canada by:
Raincoast Books, 2440 Viking Way, Richmond, B.C. V6V 1N2
Tel: (1) 604 448 7100; Fax: (1) 604 270 7161; www.raincoast.com

Part of the chapter "Learn to Breathe" appeared in another form as
"Breathing Meditation" in *Mandala Magazine*.

Part of the chapter "Move to the Middle in All Things" appeared in *The Guardian* as "Mediation, Not Litigation Swats Arguments."

The moral rights of the author have been asserted.

Cover design: Nita Ybarra • *Interior design:* Nick C. Welch

The information given in this book should not be treated as a substitute for professional medical advice; always consult a medical practitioner. Any use of information in this book is at the reader's discretion and risk. Neither the author nor the publisher can be held responsible for any loss, claim or damage arising out of the use, or misuse, of the suggestions made, the failure to take medical advice or for any material on third party websites.

To protect the privacy of others, certain names and details have been changed.

A catalogue record for this book is available from the British Library.

ISBN: 978-1-78180-285-4

Printed and bound in Great Britain by TJ International, Padstow, Cornwall.

MIX
Paper from
responsible sources
FSC
www.fsc.org   FSC® C013056

For Judy Liff Barker
with love and affection

CONTENTS

INTRODUCTION

When I was a kid, I played a board game, *Careers*, which I never won. And I played a lot. In it, players have to set their own goals for winning by allocating a certain number of points, 60 in all, to a combination of fame, money, or happiness. Most people divide the points evenly and give 20 points to each. Every time I played I put all my points, all 60 of them, on happiness. I didn't care about fame or money. I stubbornly refused to do otherwise, even when my friend's older brother explained that this made it statistically a lot harder to win. It didn't bother me that it was hard—nearly impossible. It's always been about happiness for me. I was a sensitive, possibly moody child: determined, some might say inflexible. Eventually I figured out putting all your points on happiness is a terrible strategy for winning a board game, but it turns out to be a pretty interesting strategy for life.

While my peers in college went for MBAs, I got a degree in philosophy and then in the early '80s an MFA in writing because they made me happy. In the mid '90s, I traveled across Europe and Asia, and eventually made my way to Bhutan, a tiny Buddhist country in the Himalayas, known to be a very beautiful and a very happy place. I came to Bhutan for no particular reason. I'd met some Bhutanese in New York and we'd become friends. I liked them and wanted to see their country. Bhutan didn't even show up on some maps, and my Bhutanese friends were real jokers, so there was an ever-so-slight possibility that I was going somewhere that didn't even exist.

I got myself back to Bhutan several times, and I told everyone who would listen I wanted to live here. It was really hard to pull off at the time. It still is. It's far away, expensive, and like no place I've ever known. I wasn't entirely sure why I was willing to leave everyone and everything I'd ever known and loved. But I'd had that precedent with the board game, and I'd been known to quit jobs and relationships, dismantle appliances and leave the room, burn bridges, fling skewers of shish kebab, roll over, and jump through flaming hoops, all in the quest to be happy. For me, it was the thrill of adventure and the happiness I felt when I was here that brought me to live in Bhutan. I knew Bhutan would make me a better person. ´

I didn't know how long I would stay in Bhutan. But I knew my time here would be life altering. All I had to do to realize this was fly into the country; that in itself is life altering. The Himalayas—the tallest mountains in the world—and dense jungles make a natural fortress around its perimeter, and to fly in on the nation's carrier, Drukair, is an incredible adventure and an exercise in extreme trust. Only a handful of pilots in the world have the incredible skill and guts it takes to fly here.

High up in the air, as the plane makes the approach into Paro, the runway looks like a little matchbox sitting in a field, which is sitting in a forest clearing in the middle of the most imposing mountains in the world. You are flying through a little valley with pointy mountains on all sides, and out the window you see slices of green platform fields terraced into the mountains for rice, and quaint white farmhouses that look like they're from a movie set for a little alternative Narnia-esque world. You half expect to see unicorns or dragons in the bright blue skies. You can often see rainbows. Farmers stop their work in the fields, look up, wave, and smile. You are close enough to see their teeth sparkling in the Himalayan sun.

Before the plane lands on the tiny runway, it makes a big jolt to the left to avoid a hillock with a small house on it that's next to the airport. Then the aircraft dives down very quickly toward the ground and comes to a mercifully quick stop. The flight into Bhutan gives the impression that inches, not feet, are what count. The same could be said for the journey to happiness.

Once I visited Bhutan, I couldn't wait to get back. It feels like heaven on earth. I hardly notice the hardships of living in a developing country because the people are charming and funny, and it is truly the most beautiful, unspoiled place I've ever been. And there was something else, something intangible that drew me in. Once I had a taste of it, I realized I couldn't live without it. It filled me with a sense of well-being. I liked myself in Bhutan. And because of that, I could be nicer to myself and those around me. Being kind is practically a law here because there are fewer obstacles to happiness. Life is still simpler. The country has never been colonized, and that gives the people an independent streak, a clear identity, and an optimism. They take care of each other. They laugh and enjoy life—and it's contagious. Waking up every day in Bhutan with an attitude of kindness makes so many wonderful things possible. It convinced me that kindness is the way to happiness.

Nonetheless, Bhutan isn't a place that slips easily into categories or stereotypes. It's full of surprises, conundrums, and contradictions. It is a frustrating place, a holy place, a changing place, and a hideously profane place. It smells like wood smoke, dung, clean mountain air, chilies, and incense. And if you're willing to slip out of your shibboleths and hard-held prejudices, Bhutan just might teach you some enlightening things.

I moved to Bhutan in 1997, fell in love, and married Phurba Namgay, a Bhutanese painter, three years later. In 2005, we brought a little girl, Kinlay, to live with us. It's been an incredible journey of change and adaptation: learning to live with less and more. For me, extreme measures seem to work. But don't try this at home. Or rather, try this at home. I've learned that you don't have to go to the ends of the earth to figure out how to be happy. Heck, you don't even need to leave the privacy and comfort of your own living room. It's not necessary for happiness. In fact, it might even be better to seek out happiness right where you are. I hardly left Bhutan for more than ten years, but for the past few years I've been dividing my time between Nashville and Thimphu, half a year here, half a year there. It is a heck of a commute, as far as you can go in either direction on the globe. But work, family, and life make it necessary. To keep my sanity and enjoy my life, I've put a lot of thought and energy into how to be the same person, live the same way wherever I am. There is such a big difference in the two places: how people go about their days, how people spend their time, what they think is important, how they work, play, and eat.

In the West, we have everything we could possibly need or want—except for peace of mind. We go to extravagant lengths to try to be happy. Living in Bhutan and then coming back to the U.S. has taught me that we can all learn to create a space within us where we are untouched, at our best, where we can be open to life and we can be, even in the darkest hours, calm and relatively happy. That can happen anywhere.

I've now lived in Bhutan for much of my adult life. My happiness comes because living in this ancient culture forces me to think differently—about time, work, money, nature, family, other people, life, death, tea, kindness, generosity, washing machines, waking up, and myself. Ironically, there's a lot of discomfort. But I'm happy, deeply and thoroughly. The thing is, Bhutan won't always be Bhutan. Change is inherent in all things. So when I leave I try to take these feelings and ideas I have in Bhutan with me. I call it "simulating Bhutan." Even while in Bhutan, Namgay and I have to "simulate Bhutan," because even in this quiet, relatively pristine place, we can still lose the thread.

Sometimes, we think we're happy when we feel we've achieved a sort of stability or success with our jobs, our bank accounts, our love life, and other relationships. Happiness is complicated, no doubt. It is a lifelong quest. A huge part of being happy, and the quest for it, is actually knowing you're happy, or rather knowing what makes you happy. It is deceptively simple. That's why it's so hard! That little children's song that starts out "If you're happy and you know it clap your hands," while ever so slightly cloying, is also prophetic. Happiness is harder than it looks because so many other things get in the way. So we have to simplify things, strip them down, gut the house, and then build it back up.

When I talk about happiness in this book I mean well-being. I think of happiness as being a state wherein we are "without want." Happiness is linked to kindness, compassion, having what you need, and being comfortable with yourself, but it's not necessarily linked to outward comfort. Here's what I think about happiness:

1. Everyone wants to be happy.

2. Happiness begins with intent.

3. Happiness doesn't just happen; it's a result of conscious action (and sometimes that "action" is to do nothing).

4. This action involves doing simple things well.

In short, to be happy you need a skill set. Over the years I've developed one of my own, and I've found what works for me and what doesn't. I'm a storyteller, by the way. This collection of stories, insights, impressions, and suggestions highlights things that have pushed me in the direction of peace of mind, and contentedness. Think of them as a little nudge, a push, a leg up to the top of the metaphorical mountains into the rarefied air of paradise— of bright sunlight and beautiful views.

Linda Leaming
Thimphu, November 2013

CALM DOWN

I always thought I would die in the Bank of Bhutan. No, not from an earthquake, a robbery gone wrong, or the roof caving in on the old cement building, which was recently torn down, perhaps minutes before it fell down on its own. I thought I might die of a heart attack or a stroke or from old age, or from the sheer stress of waiting for hours on end to get one teeny little check cashed. By the time the bank cashed a check it had taken so long that I needed to cash another one.

The bank's bazaar-like atmosphere made it seem more like a carnival than a bank. The smell of musty old money, chilies, spices, and dirt thickened the air. Women pulling children along and men in ill-fitting pants carrying scuffed-up briefcases, flat from being empty, raced around as if they had urgent, important business to conduct. Bank employees chewing, spitting, chatting, running, sitting, shifting papers, and carrying large ledgers and enormous pots of boiling water for tea all stopped and looked up every time a doorbell-like sound came over a loudspeaker, indicating which customers should report to the tellers. And the gentle-faced Bhutanese—mostly

I

men, but some women and children—born to endure hours, months, or years waiting at the bank, going around greeting each other amicably, shaking hands while gripping each other's forearms, created a buzzing beehive of activity that went nowhere. I halfway expected to hear circus music and see little children holding big clouds of cotton candy.

For security, an ancient guard sat dozing by the door in a khaki uniform, an equally ancient Russian rifle leaning on the wall next to him. It's one that Castro supplied to Bhutan in the 1970s, so you know it was one step up from a musket.

There might as well have been snake charmers it was all so random and chaotic, nothing like the orderly American banks of my youth, or the anonymous, efficient ATMs I'd grown to love for their discreet beeps and alerts. But instead of being amusing or charming, it all used to make my head and heart pound with frustration. I just wanted to cash my check and get on with my life.

I'd recently arrived in Bhutan to teach English at a government school, and although I thought I was pretty open to exotic experiences, in those days I was still a typical American.

We Americans are brilliant at many things: we're ingenious, we work hard, we're resilient. Even with difficult economic times, and the fact that everything and everyone has become politicized and polarized, we live well compared to many people in the world. We are energetic, interesting, intelligent people, and if I might continue to generalize, we are also the most impatient and easily addled people on the planet. We can't handle too much randomness. We pack our days with appointments and events, and even our "days off" are full of activities. In

Bhutan, if I have three things to do in a week, it's considered busy. In the U.S., I have at least three things to do between breakfast and lunch.

Living in Bhutan my stressors are different, and they involve more basic things. Food is one because getting it is problematic. There aren't many big grocery stores; Bhutan is so remote that it takes a lot of work to ship things here, so the shops aren't perpetually stocked. We have to go to many different shops to look for things we need, and sometimes things we need aren't available so we have to make do or do without. Eighty-five percent of the things I eat in the U.S.—like celery, turkey, collard greens, Starbucks, Parmesan cheese, artichokes, pecans, and pine nuts—aren't available at all, or with any consistency, in Bhutan.

Most houses aren't insulated, so keeping warm and dry is an issue. Or the flip side: we often have water shortages in Thimphu. I think these kinds of stresses (getting food and shelter) are actually easier to cope with in some ways because they are basic, fairly uncomplicated needs. Culture is also a stressor for me because no matter how long I live in Bhutan and no matter how much I like things about the culture, I have to work to adapt myself to them and include them in my belief system. Like, for example, learning to be patient and wait amidst the chaos that is the Bank of Bhutan.

Luckily, I've become better at this over the years. But what still gets me off balance is the way I think about people. Wherever I am—Nashville, New York, Bangkok, anyplace—people can make me agitated, because I secretly believe everyone in the world should just do what I say. The world would run a lot more smoothly. But that's not going to happen, and I even know it's not really true, but

I still act as if it is. The world would be horrible if everyone thought like me; my thinking gets me into trouble. I have a negative, angry thought, and if I let it, it will snowball and open the door for more negative thoughts. Before you know it I'm in a very dark mood. The other constant in my stress level is, like most Americans, I try to do too much. We're competitive, eager to please, and as a result we have high expectations of ourselves and others. This causes a lot of pressure. We know that scientific research has borne out the fact that we can't actually multitask and that our brains are incapable of focusing on more than one thing at a time, but we try to do it anyway and serially task ourselves to mental and physical exhaustion.

Our lack of calm is exacerbated in the U.S. because we want immediate gratification for everything, and we're frantic about getting it: food, entertainment, fitness, enlightenment. And things are set up so that we do get a lot of things quickly. We order takeout, text our friends, download music, and e-mail co-workers with lightning speed, and we don't even have to get out of our cars. In Bhutan, it can take an hour or more to do just one of these tasks. Speed begets speed. All of this efficiency only makes us want things faster. If we could time travel we'd get everything done yesterday so we could have today to get more done. Right?

We're not used to taking the long view, centering ourselves and making ourselves even and calm. Frankly, slowing down frightens us. The irony is that even as we want things to move faster, they often move too fast for our human brains. There's just too much to divide our attention. I am not criticizing Americans as much as I am just stating a fact. We work harder and longer than most people in the world. We take fewer vacations. And if we do take vacations, then we often do things like remodel our kitchens during them, which is, um, not actually a vacation in the strictest sense. If we don't get answers to e-mails immediately, we start to sweat. *Wait. What? It's been five minutes and my question hasn't been answered?*

We miss a lot of life by focusing on speed and efficiency, quantity versus quality, and it's stressful to live this way. An American friend of mine who visited Bhutan is a world-class runner. He and his daughter took the trek up to Taktsang, a 17th-century temple complex built on the side of a sheer cliff that is honeycombed with caves. The place was discovered by the legendary 8th-century Buddhist saint Padmasambhava, or Guru Rinpoche, who landed there when he flew on the back of a tiger from Tibet. It's iconic and a must-see for any visit to Bhutan, even though it's a somewhat difficult slog up the side of a mountain and back down again. There's an element of danger because it's so high and the trail is narrow, and parts of it take you inches from the side of an abyss. It normally takes the better part of a day to walk up and then down the cliff face, and it is a holy pilgrimage for Buddhists. If you don't have at least one thought about death—your own or someone else's—while you're negotiating that cliff face, then you're not really getting the point of the exercise. The last thirty minutes up to Taktsang is a precarious toddle down a bunch of loose stones that pretend to be steps, and then up a bunch more loose stones, around a very narrow path carved into the cliff, across a bridge over a waterfall, to the temples. It is mind altering because of the dramatic scenery, and even if you don't have anything close to a spiritual gene, you have to pause every now and then and nod to the otherworldliness and the spectacular quality of your surroundings, and take them in. You are deep in the recesses of the Himalayas, the highest mountains in the world, closer to heaven than to earth. It's frightening, beautiful, and rigorous; it literally and figuratively takes your breath away. So I asked my American runner friend how he liked Taktsang. "It was great!" he said. "We made it up in an hour and a half!" Sigh.

I'm right there amongst my fellow harried Americans, putting quantity ahead of quality. I know the feeling of not sleeping and of being overwhelmed and stressed for days at a time. And I can feel it in people around me. On some level, it's kind of fun to get worked up about things, knock things out, and be superproductive. It can make you feel alive. But it's a false sense of living because you can't be in the moment. It doesn't touch your core. You can't absorb anything. It's hard to focus. And it's not good for your mental or physical health.

In Bhutan I had to make a change pretty quickly and learn to be calm. My life here was only as good as my ability to adapt to the new culture, a new schedule, new and different food, different people, different manners, different accommodations, and a hundred other variables. Even with enormous development over the last 30 to 50 years, the isolated mountain kingdom is still a laid-back place. Life is slower, more random, and the Bhutanese sense of time is different. Perhaps the reason the Bhutanese have been able to cope with the building of roads, hospitals, hydroelectric projects, offices, and more infrastructure; the move for half of them from rural to town living; the mass education of over half of them; the move from monarchy to constitutional democracy; and more cars, business, and commerce is the fact that they take much of it in stride. They are connected to their core. It's about attitude and the ability to be centered. Even in the face of some pretty serious poverty, natural disasters, nearby geopolitical upheavals, and other casualties of living in an isolated, rugged place, they have an inner calmness that is admirable and marked. And more to the point, it's probably life extending and definitely more fun.

For the first year I lived in Bhutan, I dreaded going to the bank. As much as I liked getting money, the bank's system was beyond inefficient. First, I had to give my paperwork to someone at a desk and receive a token. It was always a different person at a different desk. There was no uniform way to get this done. Then, it was at least a two-hour wait with the token in hand in front of the teller window at the other side of the bank to sign more paperwork and finally, when the "doorbell" went off and my token number appeared on the tote board, I got my cash from the teller. During this process I'd shake my head in disbelief, sigh deeply, roll my eyes, and occasionally vocalize my irritation. Huffing. Sighing. Looking irritated. Sometimes complaining out loud. The complaining and bristling and giving everyone looks of disapproval not only got me nowhere, I think it helped lengthen the time it took to get my cash. The Bhutanese do passive-aggressive well.

I stood out, if only for my body language and my really bad attitude and grumpy red face. We don't realize until we're injected into another culture that so much of our communication is silent; we don't even have to talk to convey major attitude and lack of serenity. Unlike the Bhutanese, we wear our emotions on our face. It was interesting to observe my fellow bank customers and note that I was the only one with steam coming out of her ears. Everyone else seemed okay with the wait. They were in the moment. I wasn't. That's never a good place to be.

I had to train myself to go with the flow.

Since I was a captive audience and had to stay at the bank lest my token number was announced on the board when I wasn't there, I decided to occupy myself. I started bringing needles and wool into the bank and sitting in one of the bucket chairs in the bank lobby to knit sweaters while I waited. Have you ever seen a person knitting? It's so soothing both to knit and to watch someone do it. Like so much work we do with our hands, it is calming and grounding and deeply satisfying. It's purposeful, productive, and it connects you with history and the universe. Sitting somewhere curling wool around needles—the purposeful spirals, the rhythmic working with your hands, creating something useful—focuses and relaxes your mind. It gets you out of yourself and improves dexterity. The repetition is good for your brain. There is really nothing like it. Just ask someone who likes to garden, or prepare food, or sew, or paint. Sometimes I'd look up from what I was knitting and everyone on that side of the bank was staring, mouth-breathing, as if they'd been hypnotized by my fingers whipping the wool around the needles. It was a public service. It was meditative. And it connected me with my fellow human beings in a wonderful way. I started having conversations about what I was making, how long it took me, where I got the wool. One woman taught me how to knit a baby bootie right there at the bank. And then there was the inevitable look of surprise when they asked me to show them what I was making, and I'd hold up the sweater or stocking cap or sock, and one arm on the sweater would be noticeably longer than the other, or the socks would be hideously uneven or misshapen, because I'm quite bad at knitting, really. But the kind Bhutanese would look at my creations and beam and nod their heads in an encouraging way, and flat-out lie about how nice they looked. It was very endearing and it got to where I actually looked forward to going to the bank. To this day, if someone compliments one of the many sweaters I made, I sometimes laugh and say, "I made it at the bank."

I think we not only need to have a back-to-the-earth movement, but we also need a back-to-doing-things-with-our-hands movement. It is the most calming thing you can do. Get your fingers busy and your mind will relax and balance itself. Not only that but you'll have a finished product and a story behind it. Texting doesn't count—in fact, anything you do with a smartphone doesn't count. It makes me sad that cursive writing is a dying art. We're all up in that instant gratification thing and that need to connect that's really no connection at all. If you can get over the intense need to pull out your smartphone and pull out your ball of yarn instead, then you will be instantly connected to that warm, loving, interesting, honest glowing being that is inside of you.

For people who don't want to make fluffy scarves, finger some worry beads or a mala, sketch, file your nails, juggle, do origami, mold clay, hug, do yoga. Our ancestors did a lot of manual labor, and I remember from reading Dickens and from watching old movies how people used to wear watches on chains that they kept in special pockets sewn into the waist of their pants, or on chains around their necks. They'd pull out their watches and fiddle with them. This seems very useful. I wish it would come back.

Over the years I have learned to relax, and it's helped me embrace the absurdity that is everywhere. If you relax you can hear the cosmic laughter. Bhutan is always giving me opportunities to do this. On any given day I might have to deal with things like a spider crawling in the bed, dogs making love under my window, people dropping in unexpectedly, workmen unloading a truck in front of our driveway and blocking us in, a neighbor bringing a dead snake by our house to show Namgay, waiting more than an hour to get food at a restaurant, driving or walking all over town to find a place that sells tea we like, waiting in line for some obscure permit to travel outside of Thimphu and then finding out they've changed the procedure, dealing with crazy plumbing, or sitting in my car to catch the sun because it's the only way to keep warm on a cold winter day.

The U.S. has different absurdities. All you have to say to someone is "Life is crazy!" or "Health care!" or "Comcast!" then just sit back and listen. Everyone has horror stories of dealing with cell phone bureaucracies, negotiating traffic on Friday afternoons, air travel, bosses, taxes, politics, education, you name it.

The Bhutanese, being both Buddhist and Asian, internalize a lot of their emotions and don't express them as readily on their faces or in their actions. Westerners have been schooled in the idea that internalizing emotion is "stuffing," and it's not good. I propose a middle path. Let a few emotions go by that you don't show or reveal to others. Stand outside of your body and the situation. Try to empathize. We're all on some level just trying to put bread on the table and pay our bills and keep what we have. If you let some emotions just go by, then often they diminish or even go away.

The Bhutanese have sickness, money problems, and other worries, but as I mentioned earlier, so many of their stressors are different than Westerners'. Many don't have electricity and have to haul water to drink and bathe with. They get by as sustenance farmers, and during lean times in the year, food insecurity is an issue. If you have enough to eat, and if you have a place to sleep, if you're relatively warm, then in Bhutan you're doing okay and you might even be happy. It's a good model for us, too. Sometimes I'm ashamed of the things I get upset about because if I look at the big picture they are trivial. But the more things you have to deal with, the more stressed you become.

I learned in Bhutan that it naturally follows that to be calm you must develop an awareness of your mental states and the physical states they manifest. It seems self-evident, but as we get busier and more involved in daily things, sometimes we lose touch with our feelings and emotions. It's important to get into a habit of checking in with yourself: feel how you're feeling. If your head is throbbing and feels tight, if you have that feeling of a weight behind your eyes, if your arms and legs and back feel stiff from holding them rigid, then you are probably pretty wound up. If you have trouble focusing, if you're tapping your pencil on the desk, just note how you're feeling. Sometimes our moods catch us by surprise. We don't realize how tense we have become. Everyday stresses raise our blood pressure and affect our sleep, what we eat, what we think—every part of our lives.

Train yourself to check in a few times a day and note how you're feeling. Are you tense, angry, relaxed, calm? Check in after you've gotten a speeding ticket, after your boss yells at you, when a driver pulls in front of you and cuts you off, when you get a bill for something you didn't buy. How do you feel? But don't just focus on feelings that are negative like stress or nervousness. Check in when you're feeling good, too. How does it feel to pet your cat, to walk your dog, to hug your partner, to laugh with your friend, to work in the garden? Check in with your feelings

20 times a day. Or more. Because when we get tense and nervous and wound up, we lose the thread of how we're feeling. We have to reconnect.

Of course we mirror our environment, and this is the tough thing about living in the U.S. and trying to keep that level of calm that is a natural result of living in easy-going Bhutan. All the awareness in the world won't make you calm if you're constantly dealing with crises that happen around you. But you can mitigate the things that get you worked up. You can take a calm, critical look at the stress in your life. Structure your life so that you can at least eliminate the people or things that aren't necessary and that make you stressed and nervous.

Just realizing who makes you upset will add to your well-being and make you much calmer. Do commando visits of 20 minutes or less with difficult relatives, friends, or co-workers. You'll come out only slightly less calm than when you went in. You can do anything for 20 minutes.

And rein it in a bit. If you travel around or just observe people you'll notice that we Americans are comfortable announcing our emotional states. Many of us are good at recognizing them, too. *I'm bored, angry, thrilled, amazed, happy, sad.* Manifesting calm means just being— without announcing it. Learn to recognize what it feels like to be grounded. You want to be sensible, relaxed, and self-possessed. How people think about you is secondary to how you yourself are feeling. You don't have to tell everyone how you're feeling on Facebook. Instead, just observe how you are feeling. Or do something with your hands. That's what you're aiming for. It's the start. It will help you be calm.

If you are calm, then you are able to do more. There's evenness to your emotions and thoughts, and you will be amazed over time at what you are able to rise above. If we can learn to cope and be calm during the little disasters we have every day, then we are more able to handle the really big things when they come along. Because they are coming along. So burrow in, calm down, get in touch. Your token number will light up the tote board soon. And you'll be ready.

LOSE YOUR
BAGGAGE

My periodic bank visits aside I had very little money and even less "stuff" when I moved to Bhutan. Paradoxically, I was never happier. I remember thinking, *Oh, I need conditioner for my hair.* But I couldn't find any in the shops. So I started applying mustard oil to my hair before shampooing and using henna like the local ladies did. It turned out I didn't need conditioner. I didn't have a car, but people were really nice about giving me rides. Or I walked. It was astonishing, really, what I could live without. Almost daily I'd start a thought: *Oh, I need _____.* But it wasn't available, and so I learned I probably didn't really need it. Or I could make do with something else.

The things we carry help us or hinder us on our way through life. We all have baggage: emotional, psychological, and actual stuff for living. We need that stuff—a belief system, memories, thoughts, feelings. It makes us who we are. But God love us, most of us tend to overpack our lives and our mental closets with useless paraphernalia and prejudices that are no longer relevant to our lives.

Once I was walking out of a store and a woman walked past me wearing a silver ankle bracelet. For a split second, my inner narrator recoiled, remembering my early conditioning and my mother who told me women who wore ankle bracelets were "common." They were advertising their lascivious natures and loose morals. I laughed because I don't believe this anymore, especially since I moved to a region of the world where ankle bracelets and toe rings are the mark of a well-put-together gal. But it made me wonder if other beliefs that no longer worked were hanging around in my brain.

Wouldn't it be great to off-load all the things we don't need, that don't move us forward, and might even hold us back? Being in Bhutan taught me to make a habit of sorting through this baggage, keeping what I need and dumping periodically.

But I hadn't even gotten to Bhutan when I got a jump-start on it. By jump-start I mean I was rudely awakened.

My summons from the Royal Government of Bhutan to come and teach at a school just outside the capital of Thimphu came by fax late one night in 1997. I had been waiting for a year and a half, and I was beyond thrilled, so I paced back and forth until morning, and then I bought a one-way plane ticket across the world. Next I proceeded to sever, cancel, untie, pigeonhole, pack away, put aside, purge everything and everyone, and otherwise turn the torrent of my life into a trickle. But this wasn't even the rude awakening yet.

My friend Carly bought my kilim rugs and some tables. Rebecca carted off the sofas and beds. Carol at the gallery where I'd gotten most of my art collection kindly bought some of the pieces back. Anyone coming to visit me had to carry a box of dishes or books or clothes out of the house. I'd given myself three weeks to disengage from my life in Nashville and get on the plane to Bhutan. There wasn't much time to be sentimental. I was like a bride trying to keep it together for the ceremony—giddy, focused. I canceled my utilities and magazine subscriptions; I sold or gave away my furniture, car, clothing, appliances, computer—everything except for what I could cram into two large suitcases. Once I got in that mode, it seemed incredibly easy—almost amusing—to watch people walk away with my things, their faces bright with acquisition. Paying to store any items seemed pointless, and in fact I was on a tight budget and needed every penny since I wouldn't be making much money in Bhutan. Storage wasn't really an option. My neighbors stood in their yards and scratched their heads at the throng of takers and the parade of possessions that streamed out of my house.

"Are you moving?"

"Yes."

"Where to?"

"Bhutan. Asia."

"Which is it? Bhutan or Asia?"

"Actually it's both."

"Is it the country in Africa that's . . . ?"

"Having a civil war? No. That's Burundi. Bhutan is in the Himalayas. The mountains. Nobody's ever heard of it," I said, apologizing for the obscurity of Bhutan and for making the person feel geographically challenged.

"Oh." Pause. "Are you taking your lawnmower?"

And so it went. I whittled the last of my possessions to fit into two giant rolling duffel bags and bound them with ropes the way people did long ago when they were traveling to or from this somewhat unpredictable part of the world. Yes, in retrospect it does sound completely mad. I really don't recommend that anyone do this. It was fantastic, liberating, romantic, and so, so scary.

Saying good-byes to family and friends, believing it possible that I'd never see many of them again, upped the reality factor a bit. I ignored their polite entreaties to rethink this folly. I was focused, alone, and single-minded. I'm not sure what made me do it. I think I was in serious need of adventure. Also, it is partially the circumstances of my birth, my DNA; I like change. I like it more than most people. I decided that however long I stayed in Bhutan, it would probably make returning to my old life impossible. I felt a little sad about that, but there are trade-offs in life, I reasoned, and I was ready.

I knew that I was headed for interesting times that would lead to knowledge and maybe something close to enlightenment. I felt lucky and scared and kind of crazy, walking on a razor edge. But I also felt strong. Deciding to take this risk made me feel stronger almost immediately. What I was doing was, if not the right thing, then certainly an unusual, notable thing. Unusual worked for me.

The cheapest way to get to Bhutan at the time was on PIA, the national airline of Pakistan. Nashville to Islamabad took 32 hours with short layovers in Atlanta, Paris, and Dubai, and then there was a hop from Islamabad to Kathmandu, Nepal, where I had a two-day layover before traveling on to Bhutan, and where I had to pick up my Drukair tickets.

In Kathmandu, I got off the plane, but my two love seat–size bags didn't. That's right: the airline lost my bags. Yes, yes, baggage does indeed weigh us down. That is, unless we lose our bags in a Himalayan town in transit to another Himalayan town at the edge of the world, and then the weight of the loss of the bags is crippling. I can't tell you the angst that arose in my jet-lagged brain.

I went from one dingy, closet-size office in Tribhuvan International Airport to another, asking, pleading, filling out forms, and waiting. Emotionless Nepali faces. Smart uniforms. In this part of the world, efficiency is nil, but there are always snappy uniforms. They stamped, stapled, dog-eared, and folded the forms and either handed them back to me or used them as coasters on their various desks. I felt very alone without my stuff.

Before I knew it I'd watched several flights take off and land. I was hoping in my muddled mind that my bags might come on another flight, that some uniformed employee would race through the airport yelling in heavily accented English, "Leenda, Leenda! Come! Your bags are here!" Okay, they don't really talk like that.

All I had was my backpack filled with nothing special, not even a toothbrush. A quick inventory revealed my camera, passport, jewelry, money, a couple of books, and some water. Try as I might to stay positive, and think linearly, I couldn't see going through life with only these few things. Maybe I could buy a few things. There wasn't much to buy in this part of the world besides "antique" tourist tchotchkes—Buddhas, singing bowls, daggers. I could get several hundred suitcases full of them and not even make a dent in the supply that lined the streets and shops of Kathmandu, with truckloads more being manufactured every minute in little factories off of alleyways.

After I spent an hour at the airport filling out forms, getting my visa, and staring into space, I still couldn't bring myself to go outside to the curb, get a taxi, and ride to my hotel. How would it be to arrive for a new life in Bhutan without any luggage? I'd been ruthless, reckless even, about getting rid of stuff. The things I kept were a semblance of my life: a few books I loved, useful things like boots and first aid, clothes, warm coats, gifts, a small CD player, music, shoes, toiletries, underwear. Underwear! I'd never even seen underwear in any of the shops in Bhutan during my previous visits. I knew that village men wore homemade garments similar to briefs called "half-pants" under their traditional dress. I had no idea what, if anything, the women wore. But most of the Bhutanese women were tiny. Whatever they wore, I would not be wearing it. I brought makeup and perfume and other things I knew I couldn't get in Bhutan. I brought English textbooks to help me teach English to Bhutanese children. Crap! I was counting on those books because I was many things, but I wasn't technically an English teacher. What would I do without all the stuff? Would I ever see it again?

It was the emptiest of feelings walking out of the airport and into a taxi with only a small day pack. I felt light as air and it weighed heavily on me. I was walking, no, staggering, into the rest of my life seriously ill-equipped. I couldn't even muster the energy to be angry. I was only dazed.

Even the sights and smells of Kathmandu, the pollution and noise and intense colors, and the way crazy life happens on the streets—eating, dancing, playing music, cooking, selling, loving, walking, arguing, begging, maneuvering—didn't register. I knew smelly, loud, wet, and greasy things were going on around me, but I couldn't focus. I had wanted a big change in my life, but this was too much. I couldn't go back to Nashville. I literally had nothing there to go back to.

Without bags to fuss with, I didn't really have much to do after I'd picked up my plane ticket at the travel agency. So I did what anyone would do in my situation: I became deeply religious. I wandered around Kathmandu and visited Hindu and Buddhist temples and gave money offerings and made urgent, emotional prayers.

I still have a photo someone took of me standing next to a *sadhu,* a Hindu holy man and ascetic who has rejected the things of the world and taken a vow of poverty. Sadhus wander throughout Nepal and India and live on the outskirts of society seeking spiritual understanding or enlightenment, and they take this poverty vow very seriously. They really don't have anything; many of them don't even wear clothes. My sadhu was one of those all-or-nothing types and so he was naked except for a tiny red string tied around his hips; his wrinkly member dangled between his legs, and he had painted himself all over with red and yellow dye. His dreadlocked hair sat in a massive knot on top of his head as he puffed on a cigar-size doobie. In the photo, he looks way more composed than I do. He looks happy. Crazy, but happy. And me, still in my rumpled airplane clothes with uncombed hair, squinting earnestly, I just look crazy.

My time in Kathmandu became a confused, jet-lagged plea, to whomever and whatever, that I would see my bags again. I had unwittingly put myself in just the right position to effect some radical changes. Because there in Kathmandu, I started thinking differently about my life.

Without any physical bags to tend to, and not even a change of underwear, I was forced to think. What did I have? Mostly I had an overpowering will to get to Bhutan, to change my life, to have adventure. I'd worked hard to get myself this far. But why was I so fired up to move to

Bhutan? That was the proverbial elephant in the room. I wasn't wildly successful at writing or living or anything. I'd made mistakes. But most of my mistakes came from inaction—from not doing, not pushing hard enough, wasting time. Also, I was, like most Americans, tending toward self-absorption. That was the bulk of the emotional baggage I carried. It wasn't so much. But at times it weighed me down. There were a hundred other things I carried that are too trite or stupid or embarrassing or inconsequential to mention. But all of them together formed a past life of all of my history and thoughts and feelings—the tides and emotions that made me who I was. I knew instinctively that if I moved myself to a new and different place it would force me to focus on what's important. I didn't count on having to do it almost as naked as a sadhu.

From this day forward I would have to let go of even more stuff—emotional stuff. It was "past me" versus "future me" for the rest of my life. That time in Kathmandu, with no physical baggage and with precious little hope of ever seeing it again, did something profound to me. It was better than years of psychotherapy or counseling or drugs. I went through a fire and came out on the other side. I had put myself in a position where I'd have to work even harder to create a new life, even to survive. But I was still alive. I was still in the world.

And what of my emotional baggage? I vowed to put it on a metaphorical plane to nowhere and lose it, too—the sense of failure, the sense that my life was passing me by, the anger, resentments, bad haircuts, frustrations, slights, missed invitations in the mail. Going to a new place where you know very little and you have to reinvent yourself, why not leave a lot of preconceived ideas and notions behind, especially if they're not really working for you? That way there's room to take on more useful beliefs and ideas.

That night I didn't want to sleep. I was excited and I wanted to keep thinking because I had figured something out. We reach a point in life, through age or through experience, where more and more things we do or don't do end up a response or reaction to loss or an attempt to stave off death, that ultimate loss. Knowing this will change you. We lose things: jobs, opportunities; people die; things fall apart; opportunities present themselves and then fade; lights go out; friends move away. But then we understand that we have something at our core that makes us wake up every day and get on with it—a strength, or a guiding light, a purpose, a self-love. Our soul or essence. Our personhood. Something we can't lose. The most important thing. This realization helped me get rid of some emotional baggage. Maybe like the sadhu, not having anything but myself helped me realize my own self-worth. I had something I couldn't lose.

I owed a great debt to the airline that lost my bags. All of this rationalizing made me feel good. When I finally slept, I slept soundly.

Dawn broke as I reached the airport the next morning. I got on the tiny, white Drukair airplane with the dragon on its tail and flew to Paro. My arrival in Bhutan was a moment of pure bliss, and one for which I'd been waiting for years. A new, fresh life awaited me, and I arrived pure and if not quite sadhu-like, then pretty close to it.

"Miss, where are your bags?" said the driver when he met me.

"Lost." I held up my empty hands, my fingers outstretched. And I laughed.

Two weeks later, when I had made peace with the idea that all my stuff was gone, and had begun to collect some clothes and things I needed to live, I got a telephone call from an excited Paro airport employee. "Madam! Your bags arrived! We have sent them to Thimphu to meet you!"

My dear, wonderful, tireless father had tracked them down in the U.S. They'd missed the connecting flight and had been hanging out in some room in some dusty corner of the Atlanta airport. *Atlanta!* I felt like I'd gotten a big reprieve. I'd gone through all of the emotional work to "let go" of my baggage, both physical and emotional. And as a reward I got them back—the physical bags, that is. I took this to mean I was on something close to the right track.

I believe that at some point in our lives we each have to do what they do in Alcoholics Anonymous, that mental and emotional inventory to figure out what our real baggage is all about. I also understand that to have real passion in your life, to be excited by something, to live your life in the moment and do something extraordinary, you have to travel light. Get up and walk out of the emotional traps that tie you down. Chew off the shackles. Do it any way you can. I'm not recommending my own method, however.

Here's something interesting: Of course I was thrilled to get my bags back, and I raced home to meet the man from the airport staff who had driven them from Paro to Thimphu. I untied the ropes and unlocked the bags and my initial reaction when I unzipped the first bag was that all my stuff looked squashed and tired. Why did I bring so much perfume? Why didn't I bring a decent kitchen knife? (I couldn't find any in Thimphu.) I was glad I had brought so many shoes, but did so many of them have to be high heels? Walking in Thimphu in some of these pairs would be virtual suicide.

Without access to an endless flow of chocolate I'd already dropped a bit of weight walking around Thimphu, so the pants I packed already fit loosely. Anyway, I was wearing kiras, the beautiful woven Bhutanese dresses for women, to teach at the school. I had moved on from my obsession with the Smiths, and had found a nice cassette player and Smokey Robinson, Ronnie Milsap, and Johnny Cash tapes in Thimphu. As it turned out, I ended up giving a lot of the stuff in my luggage away.

So there you are. It's not that I eschewed creature comforts. It's just that I wasn't so attached to the ones I brought.

Pack up ideas and feelings that tie you down and send you lead-footed down the wrong path. Put them in a metaphorical suitcase and sling it over a metaphorical bridge in your mind. Let the river take them away.

LEARN
TO BREATHE

My everyday life in Thimphu consists of routines. I walk to work, school, shopping. I cook food. I clean, write, play, and sleep, all in the majestic mountains hidden away in a remote corner of the world. Not much of the outside touches. I learned to do a lot of simple things well, and that, I believe, is a secret to happiness. It's part habit, part luck, and part paring down and living simply, focusing on daily things, relaxing, and manifesting awareness. It's as easy as breathing.

I learned to breathe walking up and down the mountains. Yes, yes, I've been breathing since birth, but in Bhutan I learned that how you breathe is tied to well-being, and how you breathe can make you happier. Walking here takes stamina, sure-footedness, focus, and commitment. It's toning for your body and your mind. Walking up and down mountains teaches you to breathe and to keep going no matter what.

For the first few months I lived here I was often gasping for breath. This is a natural by-product of living anywhere over a mile high and having to go places on foot. The trek to school was at first so difficult that I woke up every morning and had to convince myself to at least make the effort to get there. I even made my peace with the idea of dying one day en route. I imagined I'd just grab my chest and keel over from a heart attack. It would be very dramatic and quick and there would be plenty of people around to see it. I made sure I always had makeup on and my hair was looking good, so everyone would be especially sorry that I was gone. If I died from exertion and lack of oxygen, at least I would die relatively young in a beautiful, exotic place. The walk took about 45 minutes, and I started out at a quarter till seven and arrived at seven thirty or so, exhausted, breathless, sweating, red of face, and alive. The last part of the walk was what did me in—a 20-minute huff up the side of a forested mountain. There was a nicely made path of cement and rocks with large steps made of boulders in the steep places. I had to stop and catch my breath about every eight steps or so, and even then I would wheeze and pant with effort after only a couple of steps. I'd be standing on the side of the trail, bent over, heaving for air, and students who lived in the hostels below, having run up and down the mountain four times before breakfast, with lungs the size of hot air balloons, would run up the trail past me. "Miss, why are you stopping?"

"Great [*heave, gasp*] . . . view [*heave, gasp*]," I'd say.

I'm sure they were on to me. Those first few weeks I'd sometimes wake up in the middle of the night gasping for air. And there wasn't any. *This isn't good*, I thought. Or it was more like, *OH MY GOD! CAN'T! BREATHE! HELP!* like someone with asthma. Maybe it was asthma. I became aware of air and breathing like I never had before, and it wouldn't be hyperbole to say I became obsessed with it. In retrospect I probably should have gone to the doctor or gone to sea level, but I kept putting it off. Lucky for me it got better. I suppose it was something like that theory of car maintenance when your car starts making a funny noise and you turn up the radio. Denial, if it doesn't kill you, occasionally works. I don't remember exactly when I was able to make it up the hill without having to stop because of the hypoxia, but it happened.

I want to pause here and give a word of advice: Don't ever do that, what I did, which is nothing. That was dumb. If you have even the slightest difficulty breathing, get to a doctor, or tell someone, or rattle some cages. You need to breathe.

The real breakthrough, the way I really learned to make use of breathing, came a few years later with something I like to call "drive-by enlightenment." In Bhutan it always seems like anytime, anywhere, when I least expect it, some random person comes up and says or does something profound. Once I thought I heard an old village man in Trongsa, someone who couldn't possibly be speaking English, say, *"That which you seek is seeking you."* In his language I asked him to repeat what he said, and it turned out he was saying something about a leaky roof. But the truth is, I get a lot of good advice in Bhutan, intended or not.

One day walking on a hill overlooking Thimphu I could see rain pouring out of the clouds on the other side of the valley, and a horizontal mist had settled in the mountain crevices. I was trying to calculate how fast the rain was traveling and how long it would be before it hit.

I decided it might be a couple of hours, long enough for me to finish my walk and get home without getting wet.

I heard a voice behind me that seemed to be reading my thoughts, "It's coming! It's coming!"

I turned around and smiled at an elegant Bhutanese man of indeterminate age who was walking briskly up the hill. He was wearing track pants and a hoodie, but his mannerisms and his whole air were so refined and gracious, I picture him in my mind's eye in an immaculate suit.

"Ah!" he said. "Feel the air! Breathe the air! You know the air is free? It doesn't belong to anybody! Isn't that wonderful?" He breathed in and exhaled lavishly.

I reflexively took a deep breath.

Nope, I thought, *none of the big multinational corporations or governments or the powers that be have yet figured out how to monetize air.* "That's true," I said. Of course they make you pay for air for your tires, but not in Bhutan, so I decided not to bring this up. Besides, I got his point.

"Feel that! You breathe in. You breathe out! The air gives ENERGY, LIFE! It feeds us!" He took another big, free swig of air, which prompted me again to do the same.

He was positively glowing, elated to be breathing. It was his meditation, he went on to explain, to contemplate breathing, the miracle of our lives, our ability to breathe and be sustained by air. "On this planet, we have the atmosphere, full of oxygen. It gives us LIFE! And I am grateful to the universe for this. This planet. My home. With air."

Our planet was fully loaded. With AIR! I'd never fully contemplated the joys of being an aerobic organism.

By now we were walking, energetically, side by side. "It's just . . ." He stopped a moment and blocked his nostrils with his thumb and forefinger, first one side then the other, and did circular breathing a few times, air in one side of his nostrils and out the other. "Ah! That's wonderful," he said. I had never met such an air aficionado.

"But think about it," he said, leaning into me and talking low, like he was saying something intimate, "how lucky we are. We are here on the earth and we have air to breathe and it fills our lungs and keeps us alive. This is how I manifest gratitude."

How marvelous is that? It made a lot of sense. Manifest gratitude for air. That's a thought. And probably if you do that enough you can figure out other things to manifest gratitude about. Something so simple as breathing becomes profound.

It's easy and free to just begin to pay attention to your breathing. I love so many things about Bhutan and this is yet another one of them. On an innocent walk one random afternoon I was waylaid in the most remarkable way by this gentleman I haven't seen before or since. It was a sort of commando raid of instruction, and it changed the way I think.

Be gloriously happy that you are human and you have air to breathe. That was my friend's message, and I suppose I had to get myself on a remote mountain to hear it, to figure it out. Breathing is also useful in and of itself as a meditation to calm your mind. The next thing to do is to practice being aware of your breathing. Breathe in. Breathe out. Do this ten times slowly and feel the flow of air as your lungs rise and fall. Feel it flow through your nose and course through your body. And then note how you're feeling. It's calming.

A year or two later I had a similar encounter and learned another meditation technique for breathing. It was during a visit to a remote monastery and a lama told me a story, transcribed here:

Here is a story. Later it will become clear to you why I am telling you.

Once there was a man who was a disciple of a great teacher, a guru of infinite learning who had attained enlightenment by breathing meditation. The man was very frustrated because he had tried for maybe 20 years to be like his teacher. But he had so many things that kept him from understanding, so many obstacles. There were daily things: his family, his friends, work, maybe he had debt, maybe he had addictions or habits that pre-occupied him so that he couldn't focus. Anyway, it was a time in his life when he felt lost, slogging endlessly and to no avail.

One day the man went to his guru and he said, "Please, you must help me. You are so wise; you can do anything. There are so many things I can't get out from under. Please help me. I feel like a drowning man."

And now you must please remember that everything this guru does, he does out of great love, as all enlightened beings do.

So to his student he said, "Yes, I can help you. I will give you a demon that will help you. Anything you ask this demon, he will do. He can help you take care of your life and make it manageable. But please just remember this: You must keep this demon busy and active. If he is not occupied every minute, then it is his nature to do mischief. He might even destroy you."

"Okay," said the man. "I will take this demon. And don't worry, because I have so many things to do every day. This demon will never be idle."

And so the man took the demon back to his house and immediately set the demon to cleaning and repairing his house. The demon fixed everything, cleaned everything in a remark-ably short time. Then he painted the house, repaired the gutters, rebuilt the garage, sorted the mail, answered e-mail—he did quite a lot. The man was surprised. He thought it would take much longer. "What should I do now?" said the demon.

So the man told the demon to help him with his accounts at his business because he had fallen behind in the bookkeeping. The demon did it.

"Fix my car." The demon did it.

"Cook some food." Done.

"Wash the dishes." Done.

"Bring me a cup of tea." And just like that, the demon brought a cup of tea.

"More food." And in no time here comes the meal.

Now the man was tired and he told the demon he wanted to take a nap.

"What should I do?" said the demon.

"You can paint the house," said the man.

"I already did that."

"Did you fix the car?"

"Done. All done," said the demon.

"Well, then, just sit there and I'll have a nap."

"But I have to do something. If I don't have anything to do, then I'll have to eat you."

Alarmed, the man jumped up from his bed. He wracked his brain. He couldn't think of another thing to occupy the demon. Or if he did think of something, the demon had it done before he could think of something else. He was panicked. He didn't want to get eaten.

So he quickly took the demon back to his guru.

"Teacher, teacher," he cried out, "please take this demon back. I can't think of enough to keep him busy. I barely finish telling him to do one thing and he's already finished it. And I try to think of something else, and he finishes that. I'm running *out of things for the demon to do and if he isn't occupied he says he is going to eat me."*

So the teacher laughed. But it wasn't a mean laugh. It was laughter of great compassion. Cosmic laughter. And he said to the demon, "You see that tree over there?"

"Yes."

"Go and climb up that tree. Then climb down. Then climb up. Climb down. Keep doing that until I tell you to stop." And so the demon did.

And here is the lesson the great guru gave the man: The tree is your breath, in, out, in, out. The demon is your mind. Occupy your mind and focus on your breathing, in, out, in, and eventually your mind will go somewhere else. And your true essence will take its place.

RUSTICATE

We can't even begin to realize how far from the natural world we live in the U.S. until we consider a place like Bhutan, where, if you have moles living in your house, you can't call an exterminator because there aren't any. It's a Buddhist country and Bhutanese don't kill, unless you really piss them off. To deal with rodents, the Bhutanese have cats and fashion litter boxes filled with rice hulls from the rice mill down the road. The rice hulls make perfectly clean, perfectly functional cat litter that's even cheaper than the store-bought kind. It's free, biodegradable, and works as a good fertilizer after the cat has done its thing on it. That, my friend, is rustication.

Twenty years ago, I was the last person you'd run into on the road "back to nature." Most probably I would have been running the other way, clutching my laptop in one hand and my flatiron in the other. I am a hothouse flower as opposed to a wildflower. But I loved Bhutan and so I got myself here and I have lived here comfortably, happily, and rather well, so that learning to live more simply and naturally among natural things was sort of a value added, like when you order a cheese sandwich and they automatically bring you a side of fries at no charge because the cook accidentally made them. It has made me and my life infinitely better and much more lively, and of course, happier.

My devolution into living more simply, and with less stuff and more uncomplicated amenities, did not happen overnight. No indeed. And it was fraught with what I can only now reflectively call travail, anguish, frustration, and a little flat-out misery thrown in for spice. I won't dwell on this, but think of the aforementioned rodent infestation and the image of coming home one night and turning on the light to behold a house that's full of God's furry, big-eyed creatures—jackrabbits the size of small children sitting on the fridge like they owned it, and mice scurrying around the floor like they're late for a party. Or imagine coming home to no electricity and no flashlight in the dead of winter late one night—when the darkness has taken on a palpable, even three-dimensional opacity—and having to stumble though the house and go outside to find the wood that is stacked up beside the kitchen door, and stumble back in—wood in one hand and the other outstretched in the void—to try to find the way to the bukhari wood stove to build a fire.

So it wasn't all sweetness and Birkenstocks and food co-ops, but I did have a spontaneous intuitive moment when I realized why it is good to rusticate. It happened during a *puja* I went to a few years ago.

Pujas are important religious ceremonies in Bhutan and every household has them. Puja is a Hindi word that is in common usage to describe the ceremonies that are called *choku* in the Bhutanese language. There are annual catch-all blessing pujas, consecrating-a-new-house pujas, long life pujas, health pujas or pujas for general well-being, and of course numerous long, expensive pujas when someone dies. Pujas can last for a few hours, days, months, and even years. During a puja, monks and lamas come to the home or temple and chant prayers and beat ceremonial drums and blow horns to appease the household deities. But the real action is in the kitchen because there is generally a lot of great food and drink at any puja, and you will most certainly be invited to some kind of celebration if you spend any time in Bhutan.

Often families will meet at their ancestral homes in remote villages. In 1999 I went with some friends to their annual puja in Wangdue, in a large old farmhouse a day's hike up a mountain from the road. There was a lot of wonderful food—rice, pork, chicken, chilies, *momo* (delicious steamed dumplings filled with cheese or meat), buckwheat noodles, and other delicacies coming to us in a steady flow from the kitchen; someone was always cooking even late into the night, and we were all eating and drinking and talking and laughing. When we weren't eating and drinking we were talking about what we just ate or drank. That's the real reason for a puja.

On a table in the kitchen there was a large basket filled with tiny, sweet oranges, and every time I passed by the basket, which was rather often, I grabbed one and ate it. These oranges literally brought tears to my sugar-deprived eyes. They were so delicious, and I want to say they recalled for me the oranges of my youth, but I never ate oranges when I was growing up.

The puja lasted three days, and on the last day, the basket empty, I asked an old *angay* (grandmother) if there were any more oranges. She laughed that laugh the Bhutanese laugh when they think I am really dumb.

"Hahaha," she chortled. "Plenty."

"Where?" I asked.

"Just there," she said, and she gestured vaguely outside. Bhutanese always say "just there." Where the hell is "just there"?

I walked outside and around the house, looking for a box or basket or storeroom or shed, something that might contain the fruit. In fact, there was nothing. I made several rounds and wandered among the nearby trees, thinking maybe they were stored there in a box or a structure of some kind.

The old woman came to the door. She was grinning broadly and gesturing. "Up! Up!" she said.

I looked up. The house appeared to be conveniently and ingeniously situated in the middle of an orange orchard, and there were certainly lots of oranges, thousands of them, in perhaps 30 or 40 trees. *I smelled them.* If I paid attention I could hear an occasional *thunk*, as fat, overripe ones fell out of the trees and hit the ground. That's how deeply and intuitively I was connected to the world around me.

Never one to waste precious time when there was food to be had, I sprang into action. One tree loaded with fruit was next to the house on a hillside, and I saw that if I climbed up the hill above the tree just a ways I could easily step into a crook where two limbs sprouted out of the trunk. So, barefoot and in a floor-length kira, I climbed the tree. Pulling oranges and stuffing them into my *hem chu*, the little pocket made by the front of my folded kira, I got a couple of dozen or so and climbed down. I put them in a basket near the house. Then I did it again.

Years ago I'd been traveling for some time in Europe and experiencing acute cathedral overload. If I saw one more vaulted arch, one more mirrored hall or sumptuous overwrought fountain with marble bodies writhing voluptuously in it, I thought I might run into an oncoming truck. On a day trip to Versailles, I left the touring hordes and wandered down a path toward the Petit Trianon, Marie Antoinette's getaway palace on the sprawling grounds of the larger Versailles. There I bumped right into Hameau de la Reine, the rustic village that Marie built near the Trianon.

She must have enjoyed the luxury she lived in, but how relieved she must have felt to come here and take off all those corsets and freakish, wide, 80-inch panniers that wouldn't fit through a door, and 40-inch powdered wigs, and Spanx and fake nails, and just exist in her loose muslin with her hair flowing, which, while still a pretty elaborate style, was positively lounging attire compared to her getups in court. The place had a working dairy, a farm, a printing press, a theater, and all the stuff you'd find in a small village. Marie Antoinette's political instincts were not great, but her instinct to rusticate was a good one, even if she was just validating popular culture and Jean-Jacques Rousseau, the French philosopher and advocate of simplicity and getting "back to nature." I was a long way, in a lot of ways, from that world; I was in a village in Bhutan. But the metaphor was apt.

Back inside I dumped the oranges in the basket on the table and took one to eat. As I ate the gloriously delicious, tart, sweet fruit I had a power surge to my cerebral cortex. Maybe it was all the vitamin C I'd ingested. *BAM!* It hit me like a thunderbolt and a déjà vu colliding on a Japanese commuter train. We're talking realization. This fruit that I'd climbed the tree to get myself, to pluck with mine own hands and harvest, this fruit that grew in this pristine lovely Bhutanese village, was the best fruit I've ever eaten, before or since, yea, verily.

I laughed. This must have been what Marie A. was after. Getting out among the trees or in a field, walking down a country lane, eating what you harvest, or sitting and looking at a beautiful view feeds the soul in a way that's so vital, so essential to our well-being. It gives a contentment that is connective and restorative at the same time. It helps us manifest gratitude. There's something intrinsic in sitting in the grass, looking up at the sky, or walking among the trees and listening to the birds and the wind. It restores your soul.

I don't hold to the notion that there's only one way into nature. Just get to a place that you feel good in, that speaks to you, where you feel free and comfortable. That's where you start. If you live in the city, get to a park. Get yourself to someplace with dirt and grass and trees. If you have a yard, make yourself a garden. Get your hands dirty. I swear, there are times when a strip of intensely green and manicured grass outside a strip mall in the dead of summer is all I have for the moment, along with one of the dreaded Bradford pear trees that are now ubiquitous along the roads and in parking lots of the American South— weak, sterile, smelly in a nasty body-odor way when it blooms, but perfectly shaped and beautiful to look at.

With nature, of course, comes not-so-pleasant creatures. Bugs are everywhere, and there are way more of them than there are of us. They're here to stay, and over the years I have changed my attitude toward them. If, when I lived in Nashville, I found a spider in the house, I would call up a big, burly friend day or night and badger him to come and kill it. Even a lowly spider can and should be dealt with on your own. First step, manifest some compassion. It is a creature of the earth just like you. You might find it repulsive, but maybe the spider finds you equally repulsive. Even a poisonous spider like a black widow or brown recluse can be dealt with in a safe, not-harming way. Trap the spider in an upside-down glass jar and then slide a piece of cardboard under the top of the jar and take it outside. Simple. I live in Bhutan with so many creatures. I can remember nights traveling in eastern Bhutan when I'd go to the bathroom, an outhouse, and the walls of the structure would wiggle with multi-legged creatures of all kinds and shapes. Another time, I encountered a bat while squatting in a toilet in Trashigang. As it flapped and swooped, I carried on with the business at hand, so to speak, while I also flapped and swooped with my arms above my head and then switched to frantically trying to cover my head, then my ass, then my head again. I couldn't decide which part needed it more.

I used to be deathly afraid of centipedes. They are so freakishly overequipped with big hairy legs and move so fast and maybe there are poisonous species. Where we live when we're in the U.S., I see at least one of them climbing a wall or scurrying across the bathroom floor after a hard rain. Before living in Bhutan for many years, this would have sent me into a panic. But now I just think, *Oh, it's you. Take it outside, will you?* Then I throw a towel over it, gather it up, and shake the towel outside.

Our house has become a no-kill zone. After living in Bhutan with the Buddhists, where every life, no matter how small or insignificant, is sacred, it feels weird to kill even the smallest bug. I was standing talking with a friend beside her car in a parking lot in Nashville and she said, "Oh look! A caterpillar!" Then she walked over to it and stomped it with her foot. *Walked over to it.* She expended energy! "What the f---?" I said. "Don't go out of your way to kill things. Live and let live."

As you rusticate, you'll encounter beauty and ugliness, peace and danger. But it will be real and of the earth. I'm an optimistic person, but deep inside all optimists, there's a bound-and-gagged pessimist sitting in the basement, struggling to get out. I believe if we don't deconstruct our lives and learn to be more earthbound and earth-friendly and sustainable, and try to live with all God's creatures, even if they're not big-eyed and behind bars in a zoo, or on our screen savers, then sooner than expected we'll be forced to, through political mandate or economics or from overuse of our resources. If Marie Antoinette had not been born the daughter of Maria Theresa, and if she'd been able to live honestly, un-extravagantly, in a village somewhere in Austria, and if she hadn't been killed by an angry mob because of her extravagances, then she'd be telling you the same thing.

DRINK TEA

When I started teaching English in Bhutan, the students were bright and eager to express themselves. I asked what they'd do during their three-month winter holiday, and many wrote they wanted to serve "bad tea" to their parents when they got home. This passive-aggressive streak surprised me until I figured out that it wasn't *bad* but a misspelling of "bed" tea they were keen to serve. In Bhutanese villages in winter when you can see your breath in the house, there's nothing more wonderful than someone you love getting up early, going outside to collect firewood, coming back in and starting a fire, brewing a little tea, and bringing it to you in bed: "bed tea"—a lovely and compassionate ritual.

I'm always amazed at the excessive number of ways to pour hot water over leaves and drink the brew. I live in the land of tea growing and perpetual tea drinking. And by default it's a land of rituals. This makes me happy. Throughout history, tea, myth, and religion have entwined themselves in Bhutan. Tea has medicinal properties, vitamins, and antioxidants; it strengthens your immune system, and was used that way in China over two thousand years ago. Then it got its groove on and became social, and because tea was originally rare and expensive, it made sense to ritualize its consumption.

Tea makes us calm but alert and focused, the perfect state of mind for meditation, visions, and prophecies, or for an afternoon doing general accounting, for that matter.

Tea was a big part of my courtship with Phurba Namgay, which began in earnest when a matchmaking friend of mine invited him to my house for tea. Over the ensuing week he kept coming back and we drank lots of it, and we eventually got around to marrying. When we moved in together that afternoon cup of tea with each other after work became a ritual that we continue to this day. Tea is so much a part of our lives, and we are thrilled when we can find the exact same teas we like in Bhutan at our local Indian grocery in the U.S. It gives us continuity and comfort.

One Saturday at lunch at a Thai restaurant with friends in Thimphu, they brought Ron, a Chinese man who lives in Malaysia. We'd met him before and were glad he was back because he was entertaining. Ron was in the import/export business and was in Bhutan to buy Cordyceps, a very lucrative business these days. Cordyceps is a fungus that grows on the back of a caterpillar, and the combined worm and fungus is said to have a wide variety of medicinal properties. The Chinese can't get enough of it. The fungus actually attacks a certain breed of caterpillar and replaces the caterpillar's tissue, which eventually kills it, but not before it grows a large spore, which looks like a blade of grass, out of the caterpillar's head. Not long ago it was illegal to hunt for moving blades of grass in the mountain pastures of Bhutan, which is where you find Cordyceps. But the king made it legal a few years ago, and now I imagine yak herders lying in the fields looking for a blade of grass that moves ever so slowly. It gives new meaning to the phrase "watching the grass grow."

Yarsa gumba is the Tibetan and Bhutanese name for Cordyceps, and it translates as "summer grass, winter worm." The ancients actually believed it was a worm that turned into a blade of grass in summer. Silly ancients. It's hugely popular all over Asia and is known as "Himalayan Viagra." Besides the, um, Viagra effect, Cordyceps helps decrease the immune system's rejection of new organs for transplant patients, and the list of other benefits is a mile long. Some people take it prophylactically in a tea each day because it gives strength and energy and wards off disease. It really is a wonder drug. Just now there's much of it to be had in the mountain pastures of Bhutan.

The yak herders in the high Himalayas are getting rich off it, and a kilo of the dried worms fetches about $2,000. A rich yak herder is different from you and me in that he's won the Bhutanese equivalent of the lottery, but instead of getting a big mansion in Beverly Hills or a BMW, he'll keep herding yak. He just buys more yak. And maybe some nice gear, like motion-sensing night cameras to track snow leopards.

Ron enjoyed lunch at the Thai restaurant, but was unimpressed with the tea. Ron comes every year to Bhutan and the Cordycep auctions, where he buys and sells tea as well as Cordyceps. He also owns a tearoom in Malaysia, and it wouldn't be stretching the truth to say he's a tea fanatic. Slim, almost hairless, of an indeterminate age, and very energetic, Ron talks all the time, mostly about tea or anything related to tea, which turns out to be everything, actually.

Ron drinks the fermented kind of tea from China, and brings parchment-wrapped, cow pie–shaped disks of tea to give us. The parchment is white and silky with red seals and Chinese writing on it. It's very nice tea to drink, and you just pinch off some of the dried tea and put it in some boiled water. During lunch Ron talked about tea and how he has made a club for disenfranchised young people who had formed gangs in Malaysia. Now, instead of roaming the streets and doing whatever degenerate activity I assume Malaysian gangs do, they come to his tearoom and drink tea.

"This tea talk is making me thirsty," I said, sitting across from Ron.

"Come," Ron said. "I will make you some real tea."

So lunch at the Thai restaurant turned into midafternoon tea. We ran a couple of errands, bought some cakes, and then reconnected at our friends' house in the hills above Thimphu. Ron had placed a tray and five small teacups on a low table in the sunroom. The cups were white porcelain with a fine blue line just below the rims, and he sat in an overstuffed chair in front of the coffee table while we sat on three sofas that lined the room. Outside the sunroom's big windows was a gently sloping lawn with pine trees and pink and blue flowers, and in the distance the mountains stood in silent vigil, adding heart-stopping beauty and a bigger-than-life quality to the proceedings.

"The water for the tea must be very hot, boiling," said Ron as a helper brought the water in a thermos.

Ron said it wasn't quite hot enough, "but anyway let's do it." Unlike our big English teapot, his pot was small and brown, not quite big enough for brewing a big mug of tea like I was used to. He added water and some loose

46

tea to the pot. "Now you see I will let this sit for less than a minute," he said.

And then he poured us tea in the porcelain cups, no bigger than jiggers for whiskey. I drank it in one sip. It was nice, nothing special, weak. He added some more water to the pot and let it sit this time for about three minutes, chatting all the time about the tea. The resulting tea had a different flavor. It was deeper, but not at all bitter. I found myself wanting more than the little sip that was in the tiny cup. Not to worry, Ron assured us. More tea would come. He added water to the pot eight times, and each time he let it brew a little longer.

"There are six mountains in China and each mountain produces a different flavor and quality of tea," said Ron, full-on holding court. He went on to describe the different attributes of each of the teas and how much they sold for in today's market. As the afternoon wore on, the light in the sunroom changed. Clouds rolled over the mountains and the sun shifted its position.

I had been in this particular room many times before, once or twice a week, over a period of about eight years when my friend Louise lived in the house. She'd recently moved and now our friends had it. Louise and I drank Darjeeling tea in the sunroom from her English tea service and Wedgwood china. I'd take a little splash of milk in the cup before she poured the tea, the English way. She drank it plain, with no milk or sugar, in the manner of true tea connoisseurs. George Orwell was one. He wrote a lovely essay called "A Nice Cup of Tea," in which he states his belief that the milk should be added after the tea, to get just the right amount. And by no means should you add sugar; sugared tea is an abomination, and he didn't much like Chinese tea, either—real tea is Indian grown. Above all, one must become accustomed to the bitter taste as well as the soothing quality of the tea.

The sunroom was all natural, hand-hewn wood with floor-to-ceiling windows on three sides, carved in the Bhutanese style. Bookcases flanked the door, which led to the rest of the house. Louise had them full of books. She also had huge jade plants, which were so large they had crossed what I assume is some kind of technical threshold into tree-dom. The heavy wooden doors that led through the dining room to the kitchen slid not very easily on an ancient metal track whenever the helper brought a tray with fresh tea and biscuits—Milk Bikis from India, which were nice to dip in the tea, and tasted like the animal crackers I ate when I was little. Louise and I would spend serene afternoons drinking pots of tea, laughing, and talking. I'm sure we discussed the most weighty of matters—births, deaths, family troubles, hopes, fears, desires, everything that life presents—but I can hardly remember anything but the happy feeling I have from the memory of those afternoons and the sense of well-being I got from them that lasted for days. I can't remember a word we said. It was like the tea erased my memory of details.

Except one day I do remember: She and I were sipping tea in the sunroom and another visitor was delivered, a little boy who lived with a government official and his family. They sent him periodically to Louise to learn a little English.

The boy, around five years old, had been brought to Thimphu from a remote village, and his family gladly handed him to the man because they knew the boy would have an exceptional life. You could spend less than a minute with this village boy and understand that he was brilliant. He had a way of carrying himself that took in his surroundings in an artless way, and an unself-conscious curiosity that put him on equal footing with everyone he met. He wore thick glasses and tilted his head because although he was gifted he was almost completely blind. He would go to Bangkok for eye treatments.

Louise has the most mellifluous voice of anyone I have ever known. In fact, she started the first Bhutanese radio station many years before. So it was right that they sent the boy to her. That day she asked one of her helpers to go to town and get a little farm set, a box of plastic animals she'd seen in one of the shops. She thought it would be nice to teach him the English names of animals he'd surely grown up with. We waited for the farm animals and drank tea.

The box arrived; we opened it and lots of brightly colored animals spilled out. We recognized pink pigs, yellow chickens, black-and-white cows, red roosters, the usual suspects. But then wait—yellow lions? White polar bears? Orange-and-black-striped tigers? This was an unusual farm.

We laughed at polar bears roaming around among the horses and pigs. Just where might this particular farm be? And what would a polar bear wrangler look like?

"Poooolar bear," Louise said and held it up for the boy to see.

"Pooooolar bear," said the little boy, his head cocked to the side, holding the plastic bear about an inch from his good eye.

How many cups of tea had I drunk that afternoon?

"The tea is collected and allowed to ferment naturally . . . we just store it in the cupboard." Ron continued our crash course in tea, tea history, and the ritual of drinking tea.

Ron said the tea we were drinking was over two hundred years old. A brick of it can cost up to $15,000. Ron's way of monetizing everything made me happy in a perverse, "I told you so" kind of way. The Chinese are clearly the biggest-spending travelers in the world right now. They don't like to admit it, but they are out-capitalizing the capitalists.

Honestly though, this drinking of tea is more than ritual. It goes all the way to sacrament. Its origins are sufficiently ancient so that its history has monkeys and myth and dragons featured in it. It seems like long ago people didn't draw such a line between reality and myth, or reality and idealism. Or is it the tea itself that has some kind of mystic, charmed quality? On any given day I'd be hard-pressed to describe reality except for my own immediate situation, but sitting in the sunroom on big overstuffed sofas, my mind went into overdrive.

"This teapot is very old and worth a lot of money," Ron said. He had a Dutch friend in Malaysia and the two of them do business recovering the tea paraphernalia from big Chinese junks that sank hundreds of years ago. The Chinese government sells the rights to hunt for them. The junks carried tea from China to the New World from the 1600s on. Ron also indicated that the cups we were drinking from had come from the bottom of the ocean and were likewise quite valuable. At the time the pots and cups were made, tea was rare and quite expensive, so that's why they were so small.

Thousands must have sunk from storms, or been plundered by pirates. So this teapot was centuries old, rescued like many others from the bottom of the ocean and sold to newly rich Chinese in Shanghai or Beijing. "It's quite valuable," he said again, calling attention to the price, showing his big teeth, and waiting for someone to ask him exactly how valuable.

But no one did. We were saturated with tea and with the values of other things we couldn't fathom or didn't care about. Besides, this was Bhutan. Once I asked a Bhutanese friend what he'd do if he had a million dollars. "I would buy roller skates for my dog," he said, laughing.

Ron switched topics and talked about a mutual friend, a Malaysian who carried around a camera bag filled with six teacups, an electric water boiler, a teapot, and of course tea. He's never without his bag. I tried to imagine being so obsessed with anything that I'd want to carry it around. I don't even carry my cell phone around.

It was a lovely, lazy afternoon of drinking tea out of cups that spent three centuries at the bottom of the ocean sitting in a waterlogged, barnacle-encrusted crate in a Chinese junk bound for Boston or New York.

I know I'd drunk at least ten cups of tea, but after that I lost count. Definitely something was happening in my head, though. Tea is a drug, after all. I was in a dreamy state where my thoughts were slow, but they seemed sharp and vivid. I could taste their flavors, sweet, tangy, rich. I was thinking of colors: the blue of the ocean, the rich blue of the Asian sky, white clouds, white rice, white teacups, and storm clouds brown as the teapot on the coffee table in front of Ron, which started drooling water gently and almost imperceptibly. But as I watched it, the flow became steady and strong until it was like a full-flowing waterspout. Water spewed onto the floor quickly, like in the cabin of a sinking ship; the room began to fill quickly with water; the water swirled and lifted the furniture, which floated by and flowed out the window, reclaimed by the ocean that had replaced the mountains and pines outside.

Now we were all sitting at the bottom of the ocean, open mouths emitting bubbles, but no sounds. Farm animals floated by, and then a polar bear swam by, his thick black claws groping the water.

The ancient ritual of drinking tea—or if you prefer you can just think of it as a social activity—has some magic to it. Maybe it's just that it makes you slow down and pay a little attention. Maybe it's because it's nice to do with friends; it's a way to connect. Maybe it's more of a drug than we think. Either way, it makes me so happy to drink tea.

Here are my suggestions on how to get the most out of tea:

1. Turn off the television, computer, phone.

2. Find that mug or that teacup you like.

3. Boil water.

4. Put a tea bag in the cup.

5. Pour in the boiling water. It's important for the water to splash over the tea and wake it up. Let it steep for a minute or two. If you put a little saucer over it, it will suffuse the water nicely.

6. Sit down. Drink.

7. Now, this is the hard part: Don't do anything else. Finish the cup of tea. And don't put any sugar in it. Drink it as it was meant to be drunk. Let the bitter taste be a reminder to manifest compassion for all beings chased by karma.

KINDNESS
WILL SAVE US

Namgay characterizes people according to the condition of their hearts, as in "His heart is good," or "His heart is black," or "Her heart is small like a baby's." If someone has a good heart but "acts funny," it means that person did something rude or churlish, like hit his car and ran away, or overcharged him for something.

I think people are all basically the same. We are neither good nor evil, but we do varying degrees of kind things out of awareness and compassion, or unkind things out of thoughtlessness or ignorance.

"Help but don't hurt," the Buddhists say, and living for so many years in Bhutan, it's become part of my beliefs. Here it's not difficult to cultivate awareness of the people around you and do something helpful for someone every day. In a small society, almost every action is noted. Kindness is the glue that holds Bhutanese society together. I've seen strangers buy a meal or give a lift to an elderly person. Adults stop their cars, get out, and instruct groups of children about traffic safety.

Anywhere we live we are part of a collective conscious-ness where we must cultivate kindness for ourselves and our community. It's never been more important. To cul-tivate benevolence we have to let go of anger and think of other people.

A few years ago in Bhutan I was at the Uma, a beautiful hotel on a hillside in Paro, having breakfast with John, the hotel's manager. He ordered a three-minute egg. When the waiter delivered the egg, John tapped the top off and the egg was raw.

He laughed. "This happens all the time in Asia," he said, putting the top back on the egg and looking around for the waiter. "People here don't generally eat three-minute eggs. The cook put the egg in a pan of cold water and then put it on the stove for three minutes, as opposed to putting the pan of water on the stove, bringing it to a boil, and putting the egg in the boiling water for three minutes."

"That's why I don't eat eggs," I said, vaguely interested. I took the last sip of my coffee.

John got the waiter's attention by smiling at him, and when the waiter came to the table, instead of registering disapproval, which is sort of what I expected, John was overly bright and cheerful. He spoke in a low, conspira-torial tone, not calling attention to himself or the waiter. The restaurant was full of tourists.

"I'm so sorry," he said. "I've ordered the wrong thing. Please tell the cook to *please* put some water in a pan. If it's not too much trouble, ask him to please let it come to a full boil, and then drop the egg in the water for three minutes. That's how I want the egg. Please say how very sorry I am to have inconvenienced him." Then he smiled again.

The waiter nodded and turned to me. "I'll bring you more coffee."

"Thanks," I said, and he walked toward the kitchen with John's plate.

"Um, what just happened?" I asked.

John waved his hand dismissively. "It's an Asian thing. The cook messed up, but why say it? You know. Saving face. And I didn't want to kill the messenger, because he's just bringing the food."

"So instead of pointing out the mistake, you implied it was your error and could he please indulge you this one time and fix it, because you're such an idiot? That's awesome."

"He can tell the cook I made a mistake, and then he can tell him how to cook the egg. The waiter knows. The cook will figure it out."

"You're brilliant," I said. "Also, they won't spit in your food."

He grimaced.

Face-saving is an exercise in kindness. It means you don't yell and get angry. Sometimes you even take the fall. I realize this will be impossible for some people with instructive and highly volatile natures—I mean Type A's of course. If this is the case for you then you should spend as little time as possible in Bhutan. It's almost a given that you won't get exactly what you want there when you order food in restaurants. And if you're hostile, you might get more, if you know what I mean.

Like everywhere, there are many layers of behavior in Bhutan and there is a hierarchy, but the bottom line is that everybody makes an effort to be civil and help everybody else save face. If you're a foreigner, you'll be shown respect and dignity, and everyone will be nice. It is considered the ultimate bad manners to raise your voice, show anger or call attention to yourself in a negative way, complain, or make a spectacle. Strong displays of emotion are not shown in public. Anger, especially, brings loss of face to the angry person as well as the recipient.

Saving face is about civility, and civility and kindness are important markers for quality of life. If we go around unable or unwilling to put ourselves in other people's shoes, and lack the empathy to show respect and give people a modicum of dignity, then we are lost. We should conduct our lives and our interactions with everyone so that we show respect. Even if you secretly don't think someone is worthy of respect, at least act like you do. Everything from foreign policy to interactions at the grocery store will be better for it.

Like saving face, giving is ubiquitous in Bhutan and a big part of being kind. At the macro level, gift giving is simply engagement; it is showing other people you care, and it's an important way to interact. In Bhutan, everyone always brings a gift when going to someone's house. It's part of the social construct, and an expression of goodwill. The gift is often food such as eggs, butter, biscuits, vegetables, or alcohol. Most of the time it's just a token, and it's not the expense or lavishness of the gift that counts. It is the symbolic nature of the gift, confirming you are a member of the community and you do what everybody else does. Gift giving can also be a complex interaction, depending on things like frequency and value, who is giving and who is receiving. It often enhances the giver more than the receiver, because there's power in being generous and magnanimous. Besides being an indication of wealth, it can put the receiver in a situation of owing.

An American we knew came to Bhutan to work for a few months, and I told her that if someone invited her for dinner, she should take a small packet of biscuits as a gift. It would have cost the equivalent of a dollar in American currency, but our friend wasn't raised to bring gifts and didn't feel that it was really necessary. She never once did it. She complained later that her Bhutanese friends had stopped inviting her to dinner. It wasn't that people wanted her to lavish them with gifts. When she refused to do as was the custom of the society, she effectively cut herself off from going any further in the culture. So in this way, gift giving is a marker, indicating you go along with the customs.

Another lovely "giving" habit is when you go to someone's house in Bhutan and you're automatically offered some tea. I think it's so funny when we're in the U.S. and Namgay asks the man who comes to read our meter, or the plumber, or the fumigator if they want some tea. I always watch their reactions. They look at him like he's offered to pour sand down their boots, or sometimes they look momentarily shocked, like he's suggested they do something perverted to our cat. They receive his offer with a mixture of confusion and embarrassment, like prisoners who are being treated well by a prison guard. "No thanks," they say briskly. I love the custom, and wish when the plumber comes to fix the sink we could sit down together afterward and have a cup of tea and some cake like we do in Bhutan. I could find out about him and his kids, chat him up, laugh a little, have a nice break in the day. It's so civilized.

I am so used to the saving-face dance, gift giving, and other rules of etiquette after living so long in Bhutan, that I inadvertently act the same in the U.S. It's a lot harder, though, because almost no one "gets" Bhutanese manners. We're accustomed to some pretty rude behavior in the U.S. because we often have only superficial interactions. And we're too busy to wait patiently to get our eggs cooked just the way we like. We have so much stress.

We are more apt to express displeasure in the U.S., but what if we didn't? Ninety percent of the time the salesperson you're complaining to doesn't make the store's policy, and the server has very little control about how the food is cooked. Service people in general are the foot soldiers—underpaid, overworked, and possibly unhappy—and so complaints made to them beat them down even more. Most are just trying to get through the day, hang on to their jobs.

In the U.S. we have a tight, tense, difficult time managing everything we need to manage, and, sad to say, we feel anything from annoyance and irritation to flat-out rage on a daily basis. Anger is a sort of poison created by fear; it's a way to protect our egos when we feel threatened, and if we can't let go of anger and resentment, it turns to hate. Hate is what's wrong with the world.

There's an ingenious Buddhist practice, a meditation technique, to help disengage from anger. It's a way to alter one's mind-set, manifest calm, and get free from anger so that kindness has room to come in. Here's what to do: When you feel angry, don't try to calm yourself at first. Go the other way. Go crazy with your anger—at least in your mind. Remember, you're not acting on any of this. You're just meditating. You're angry your boss criticized a project you spent months on. You feel she did it out of a need to sabotage you or your work. Go ahead and feel that feeling of anger; feel it, and then feel it even more—really amplify and exaggerate it. *How dare she! This is the worst possible thing that could have happened to me! I hate her! She must be punished!* Now get creative. Imagine her awakened in the dead of night, arrested in her ratty old pajamas, going on trial; visualize her going to prison. Send her to Texas and let her be electrocuted. Visualize it playing out to the next level, and the next. Your fantasy will reach a level of absurdity or violence or both until the anger deflates like a balloon. It takes practice, but eventually you can learn to control anger. Then you can move on to doing other enlightened things.

Once I needed wireless Internet for a temporary stay in the U.S. We didn't want a contract; we wanted a "pay as you go" plan. I prefer the uncomplicated phone and Internet service in Bhutan because all you have to do is bring a phone in to one of the providers, and they'll put a SIM card in it, and you're good to go. You can buy as little as two dollars' worth of minutes to use the phone. Pay now or later. And they're not picky at all about the devices. They can rig anything. I believe if you took two cans and a string into Bhutan Telecom, they'd try to load a SIM card on it. They would definitely give it a try.

I went to a place in Tennessee—I don't want to name names . . . let's call it "Horizon" —and the first thing the salesman did was ask for my driver's license so that he could put my information into a computer. He was a large man wearing an even larger red shirt that flapped and billowed and made his arms look tiny like a puppet's. I brought my laptop to connect the device at the store, but there was a problem and for whatever reason, he couldn't find a unit that would work. He opened three different boxes with three separate devices, punched some buttons on the computer, made numerous phone calls to an office on a mountaintop somewhere in Bulgaria or Mongolia, sighed a lot, and after two hours, suggested I come back in a couple of days.

He was having a bad day. Why didn't I leave sooner? By God, it's because I'm an American from the land of "get it right now," and I wanted my birthright. I went across the street to another phone company—we'll call it TI&T. That company's device worked right away.

A few weeks later I started getting bills from Horizon for this service that I didn't have. *Wow, I knew these American phone companies were strict, but billing for just coming into the store and* trying *to get service?* Their service wasn't great, but their accounting sure was super efficient.

I rushed to the Horizon store. The salesman I'd worked with wasn't there. Then it started to get surreal. The store started to fill up with customers, and three separate salespeople gave three different answers to what I should do. There was an element of deep despair and resignation in their voices.

"It's going to take you at least forty-five minutes on the phone to get this straightened out [big, dramatic eye roll]."

Me: "For ME to straighten it out? I have to call? Can't you just delete me from your computer? I don't even have the service. Your records will show that."

Eye roller: "No, it's with Corporate now," he said ominously. "We're not connected to Corporate. You'll have to call."

This raised all kinds of questions, but I said, "May I use your phone?"

Eye roller: "Mine doesn't work. Use that one." He gestured to an empty desk at the other end of the store. This being a service provider for a multinational telephone company, wasn't it highly ironic that the telephone at his desk didn't work? *Was he just trying to get rid of me?*

It was a dreary place. Around the perimeter of the store, the salespeople stood in front of computers at red blob-shaped counters reminiscent of something out of *The Jetsons*. They couldn't sit down.

I was frustrated and mad but keeping it together. No one was helping. I thought about tearing up the bill, but if the company kept sending them and I didn't pay, I was worried it would mess up my almighty credit rating. I was in their system. It had reached a Kafka-esque level of absurdity. I'm all for absurdity, but I didn't like how I was being shuffled off. I wanted to yell at somebody. I looked around and everyone averted their gaze like I was an untouchable. Even the handful of customers in the store standing with salespeople or waiting their turn to be served were giving sidelong, worried glances. *Why weren't there any chairs?*

"I'm not even a Horizon customer," I whined to no one.

Of course they didn't want to deal with me. Everything was geared to signing people up with services. Signing me up was the one thing the salesman seemed able to do, but there was no one anywhere near the customer service counter in the center of the store, and no way to easily correct a glitch like this one. All were salespeople and most likely compensated according to how many people they plugged into devices.

This is what is wrong with the world! Anarchy now!! Anger was making me feel like a stranger to myself.

I needed to get calm and try not to incite anyone. I saw that they were already defensive, expecting me to explode. Anger wouldn't help me sever my weird connection, which was really no connection, to this phone company. I took deep breaths, found a phone, and dialed the service number. Holding the receiver to my ear, I moved through the menu of options and was put on hold for what seemed like ten hours, forced to listen to jazzy adverts for more Horizon services.

Mother of all that is divine and holy! How much of this can a person stand? I could feel my heart rate accelerating. The more I listened to the glib adverts and sleek canned music, the angrier I got. *More services? I don't think so. I'll show you more services!*

Then, standing with the receiver to my ear in the corner of the store, I visualized my pudgy, middle-aged self, dressed head to toe in black like a ninja, my face covered so only my eyes showed. In one hand I held a sword, which I brandished liberally, in the other, nunchuks. I leapt up on the eye roller's desk and kicked him in the face.

"Ooof!" he went and fell backwards, grabbing his nose. I'm sure it was broken, but his hair stayed in place nicely. Women waiting to sign up for the latest iPhones clutched their children and screamed in terror. "That's right! Run away, little sheep! Ahh-hahahahaha! No iPhones today!" I said, and it appeared as a subtitle at the bottom of my visualization, like in a Chinese kickboxing movie. Defying gravity itself, I did a flip in the air and leapt onto a counter, hurling the sword toward the back of the store. There was a crash, and boxes of phones spilled out of the doorway of their stockroom. I retrieved and hoisted the sword. A subtitle came: "Free Samsungs for everyone!"

I was startled awake when an actual man's voice came on the other end of the line. I explained I was being billed for a service I hadn't signed up for.

He said I *might* be able to get a credit.

"Might get a credit?" I repeated. "What about definitely get a credit? That sounds better." I knew he was reading from a script, or was trained to give certain responses. But this was so frustrating and demeaning. It's like not actually talking to a person, or being treated like a person.

"Let me see what I can do."

After a moment he came back. "You'll need to talk to someone in Loyalty."

"Loyalty," I snorted. "Okay. But that sounds a little Orwellian." He didn't respond to my remark, but immediately put me on hold. *Jerk!*

I'd been in the store 40 minutes. *Forty minutes of my life I'll never get back*, I thought. This could go on for hours, weeks, months. I remembered a song my father used to play called "M.T.A.," by the Kingston Trio, about Charlie, a man who didn't have enough money to pay the fare increase on the subway, so he had to stay on the train forever. I remember being amazed that Charlie's wife came down to the station every day to hand him a sandwich as his train zoomed by. Maybe Namgay would bring a sandwich to the Horizon store.

This is a big load of crap!

"Okay, I'm connecting you now," said a voice on the other end of the line.

The man I spoke with in Loyalty couldn't resolve the problem. I hung up. Then I took a deep breath and begged yet another salesman at the store to help me. He took a stab at calling someone at another Horizon office. They put him on hold. He got cut off.

Then I started to think out loud. "I am so sorry," I said, meaning it. "You have a really hard job."

The salesman exhaled a huge breath. "You don't know the half of it," he said.

Then he offered me a chair. *Where had that come from?* He would talk with someone else in the store, he said, and they would figure out what to do. He was gone a few minutes, and when he came back, he sat down and concocted a letter on his computer that he e-mailed to someone, somewhere in the bowels of Horizon, and so far I haven't received another bill.

So that was it. The whole situation shifted when I said a few kind words. That's really all it took. Looking back, I realize from the moment I entered the store I was probably projecting a whole lot of attitude. A little kindness went a long way. That and my awesome anger management.

On a fundamental level anger protects our egos. We get angry when we're fearful, when we think we're losing control, or when we can't handle the real emotions we're feeling. So the first thing to do to be kinder to the world is to manifest kindness and compassion for yourself. That's really the key. As you gradually begin to manifest compassion for yourself, then you naturally begin to have compassion for other people. It's a matter of cutting through the anger and fear and most of all, forgiving ourselves. Then kindness feeds itself.

IT'S OKAY TO
BE WHO YOU ARE

It's funny how life is slower here in Bhutan, but in some important respects, it's speeded up. Realizations, comprehension, awareness, recognition—whatever you want to call what happens when you acquire skills—are faster when you're part of life's natural rhythms, with slower, more purposeful work, time on your hands. It's a great way to become comfortable in your own skin, and you have time to understand who you are in relation to the world around you. That's why it's okay to be who you are. It's the way to learn to love yourself.

Musing about nature, and by that I don't mean sitting back and taking instruction from the rocks and trees, or sitting in a cave somewhere, or playing in a meadow with unicorns, but paying attention to the profound things you learn about yourself if you pay attention to nature is powerful. And guess what? You are nature. Nature is you. That's right. Whether you believe we have dominion over the world's creatures, or you're not so much into the hierarchical, dominating side of things and are more into harmony and "live and let live," you and I, as human beings, are part of the natural world. But we humans can be pretty hostile to it—with polluting, fracking, overdeveloping, overpopulating (seven billion of us on the earth now), wars, Walmarts, and whatever else our bad selves can manifest to kick Earth's ass and use it up . . . which is really our *own* ass. I think we do it because of that weird dominion thing. And greed. Anyway, I don't want to dwell on how aggressive we are. I want to dwell on that other side to our natures, the part of us that can live in harmony and appreciate and thrive in nature with our body and mind working together, teaching each other, in tandem.

Learning is my life, and not my last name, like some people who might need glasses think. I had so much to learn when I first came to Bhutan, and I was ready—more than ready—willing, and somewhat able. I assumed the position of student. I knew I'd have a steep learning curve—one straight up and off the chart. Every day was like walking into a minefield of confusion, social gaffes, and general confrontations with the aforementioned natural world, a sort of uninformed, Netflix-watching, unconnected kind of suburban woman stumbling in the wilds—a *Green Acres* thing, and not so much Walden Pond or *Avatar*. I was overwhelmed and puzzled, baffled, mystified, or bemused about 90 percent of the time, and I stopped just short of wandering into traffic or falling off a cliff. My Bhutanese friends were helpful in that respect. Habits, hygiene, traffic, food, everything was confusing. But as I've said before, that is the exact right state to be in so as to effect a great deal of change and learning. It was fine, really.

The first years of our marriage, Namgay and I lived outside of Thimphu on a little farm, and someone gave one of our neighbors, Pema, a racehorse from Calcutta. He was a beautiful animal, bred to race, with sleek muscles and impossibly long legs that looked like they would snap if the wind blew hard. Being from India, he naturally didn't do well in the mountains of Bhutan.

Pema would bring him to our house so I could ride him in the flat fields. Born and bred to run in big circles and try to get out in front of a bunch of other horses, he was the exact opposite of the Bhutanese ponies that are bred short, stout, nimble, willing and able to carry big baskets of stuff on their backs and teeter on precipices and rocks, and follow their leader in an orderly group through the mountains. Pema made a little paddock for the racehorse to exercise in, and things were going okay, until he tried to get the horse to walk up a hill. The horse had never seen a hill, had never encountered anything but the flat world of racetracks and beautiful green meadows near Calcutta. He balked and whinnied and bucked Pema like a rodeo horse. I've never seen a more perplexed look on anyone's face as was on Pema's. He led the horse away rubbing his backside, having landed on it, mumbling something in Sharchop, the language of Eastern Bhutan. Later I asked Namgay what he said. "A horse isn't a horse unless it can walk up a mountain, and a man isn't a man unless he can walk down," he said. True that.

As much as Pema admired the beautiful animal, he couldn't bring himself to do anything much with it. He was kind to it and treated it well and fed and brushed it and gave it medicine, but the horse was of no use. It wasn't even a real horse in Pema's eyes. He was just as lost as the racehorse. He'd never been to Calcutta or seen a horse race;

this wasn't part of his world. Sadly, the racehorse eventually foundered and died. He ate some grass that swelled his belly, and it killed the poor animal.

So what did we learn here? Yes, that's right. If you're a racehorse, don't come to Bhutan.

I kid. I'm sad the horse died, but the Buddhists would say it was his karma. It gives a little comfort to think that way. There's not a lot you can do about the cycle of life and death. Attachment is so very painful. It strikes me that we are all, for the most part, naturally and culturally bound. We can't get out of it, really. I'm not comparing myself to the racehorse per se, but I can certainly understand being in a place that is completely alien to any place you've ever known and not knowing what to do. For example: me every minute in Bhutan.

Soon after the death of the racehorse, although not at all related, we found out my mother had cancer. I did what anyone would do half a world away hearing that news and lacking the money for plane fare. I lit butter lamps in the temples all over Thimphu, Changangkha, Dechenphu, and anywhere else I could think of. I prayed. I cried. I bargained with the universe.

Pema kindly offered to help me put prayer flags up for my mother on the mountain above our house. The flags have Buddhist prayers written on them and Buddhists believe that the wind carries the prayers up to heaven. Recently, I was helping my father go through some things and found a framed picture of Pema I took the day we raised the prayer flags. I'd photographed him while standing above him on a mountaintop; long tree trunk poles lay on the ground. He'd already dug some holes and cemented three into the ground, so the multicolored flags have the mountains as a backdrop. I caught a moment when Pema looked like he was dancing with one of the enormous poles as he hoisted it. It is so graceful and beautiful to see the colorful flags, the mountains in the clouds, and the handsome, wiry Bhutanese man, and it doesn't look like something a sweet Presbyterian woman a million miles away would have on the table beside her bed, but she kept it there until she died.

After that, it seemed like Pema took me on in much the same way he tried to train the racehorse to go up the hill. Early one April morning, Namgay and I awoke to the sound of digging in our backyard. It was early, just after dawn, and Namgay got up and looked out the window. "Uh-oh!" he said.

That's never good to hear. I jumped out of bed and as my eyes focused I saw Pema in the garden furiously plunge his shovel into the earth and scoop up my beautiful yellow corydalis. There was a pile of wilted flowers he'd already uprooted, new spring growth, lying over in one corner of the yard, and he was making his aggressive way to the other end of the garden with the rusty shovel.

I had wanted the house because of the garden, small and rectangular, bordered by a waist-high stone wall. It was about 30 by 50 feet, just the right size for my unambitious puttering, with a small stone patio on the side, shaded by peach trees. I had a lot of flowers in it and it was a bit wild and disorganized, but I loved the way things came up haphazardly. There had been other gardeners before me and so I let the ghosts of their gardens come out. Namgay always wanted to go in and prune it. But I complained so much he eventually gave up.

"What the hell?" I said. "What's he doing? Has he lost his mind?"

"I don't know. Are you okay?"

He knew how much I loved the garden. He ran downstairs to make some emergency tea, and I stayed upstairs and paced, listening to Pema dig. I couldn't bring myself to look again. By seven o'clock, he'd turned over all the soil, fertilized it with good manure, replanted the flowers in impeccably straight raised rows, and watered everything.

I was having all kinds of feelings. I was sad, devastated really. I don't like flowers planted in rows. I felt violated. Shocked. Puzzled. How would you feel if someone came in one morning and dug up your garden? I knew that Pema was doing it out of kindness, which is the place everything he does comes from. That's why I didn't run downstairs and make him stop. A small part of me, the smallest available part that wasn't horrified, was amused, charmed even. He must have thought there was something terribly wrong with me that I couldn't plant flowers in a straight line, that I had some kind of gardening dyslexia. To my mind, my garden was marvelous—a little chaotic, but full of color. The intense Himalayan sun and plenty of water will allow just about anything to grow. Pema must have gritted his teeth every time he passed by this mass of flowers blooming messily: carnations, zinnias, marigolds, alyssum, morning glories, iris, and many things I didn't bother to find the names of. In the summers a cuckoo bird came to live there and drove everybody crazy with his monotonous song. He didn't like the neat rows either and he never came back. I decided he was charming and so I missed him, too.

Pema was a former military man, a sergeant in the Army, and so he liked precision. Once I heard someone make a joke about how to get along in the Bhutanese Army: if it doesn't move, paint it; if it moves, salute it.

Something like that must have been going on with Pema. If it's a flower, plant it in a straight line.

It would be absurd to imagine this kind of thing happening anywhere else. People in other parts of the world tend not to poke in each other's gardens. It would probably make headlines in the U.S.: "Man Assaults Neighbor's Garden in Early Morning Raid." Lawsuits happen with less impetus.

A few days later, I saw Pema walking down the road and I called him to come for tea. I hauled out a big thick book called *European Gardens* that I'd brought from the U.S. and gave it to him. The photographs and prints of stately old gardens, topiaries, magnificent displays of color—with quite a bit of symmetry, and even a bit of randomness—amazed him. He'd never seen anything like it. I wished I could have gotten him a subscription to *Military Gardens Quarterly*. Actually, there's no such publication. But wouldn't it be great if there were?

Pema's reorganization of my garden was useful when the peaches were ripe. We had five fertile peach trees in the garden, and during late summers, I collected and distributed maybe two hundred pounds of peaches. If they stayed on the ground for very long, they went bad or bugs would eat them, and the sun would ferment them within a few hours or the rain and mold would get them. If I missed a day and didn't collect, we'd wake up to the smell of rotten peaches. With my tidy new garden it was easier to scoop the bad ones up off the ground and pitch them over the stone fence for Pema's bull to gorge on. If the cowboy let the cows out early and we were still in bed, the bull would come, like a spoiled pet. I could hear him snort and stamp through the open window. When that didn't work, he'd start to bellow.

"Your friend is calling you," Namgay would say.

I tried to ignore the bull—it was too early to get up— but I knew he wouldn't stop until I dumped some peaches over the wall.

The bull stood all day beside the wall while I was in the garden. He let me scratch his back with a garden rake. I felt okay about it as long as he was on one side of the stone fence and I was on the other. I wanted to try to fatten him up, to make him healthy and virile again. He was old and his mangy hide hung on his spine like one of those Australian oilskin coats. Sometimes when I was weeding and he was standing on the other side of the wall, I'd hear this great gush of water. He was having a pee.

In India, they feed cows a steady diet of mangoes and mango leaves so their urine is bright yellow. They collect it (I don't want to think too much about how), dry it, and make paint out of it. Namgay has some yellow pigment from India that is made from cows' urine.

I'd have to watch out for the bull when I went to weed or pick the vegetables we planted behind the rice mill on his side of the farm, and I had an exit plan. If I was there and the bull stood sideways with his back arched and his head down, I slowly backed away from the tomatoes and moved toward safety, because he was in charging posture. We put a wooden box next to the wall so I could run backward to the box and jump on the wall to the other side; no running with my back to him as that incites a bull.

He was a dairy bull and they are more aggressive than beef bulls, though sometimes he'd ignore me altogether. He was a bit random that way.

I had grown up with Ferdinand, the beloved children's book character and the love bug of bulls who didn't want to fight in a bullring; he wanted to smell flowers. I wanted him to be Ferdinand, but this bull was no Ferdinand.

Still, I thought if I named him he'd be less aggressive. It sounds like I was insane and had too much time on my hands, and yes, I acknowledge the possibility of one or both of those things. I looked up names of rodeo champions: Troublemaker, Babycakes, Tombstone, Dr. Hollywood, Nightlife, Gentleman Jack, Showboat, Extreme, Super Dude, Maximum Overdrive, Boy Howdy (a.k.a. Son of Bodacious), Rotten Cotton, Iceman, Happy Ending, Mission Control, Black Magic, Milky Way.

Namgay saw the list and begged me not to name the bull.

"Why does he get mad at me?" I asked Namgay. "I feed him peaches. I scratch his back."

"I'm not sure he's mad at you," he said. "He's a bull. That's what bulls do."

I don't know why I was so adamant to domesticate him. I thought I could tame him, that he understood quid pro quo, like dogs seem to and cats understand but ignore. If I fed him peaches and scratched his back I felt as though he should have the courtesy not to charge. Now I understand that he was just doing his thing. Bulls have no morality or civility. They are just bulls, like Namgay said, doing their aggressive, dumb, bull thing. The older they get, the meaner they are, which isn't unlike some people I know.

I thought I could trump nature with nurture, tabula rasa; the bull's mind was a "blank slate" and I could train and mold him. I was giving him way too much credit. But I was the one who was naïve.

At the beginning of the summer, the bull was thin and frail. During peach season, he filled out and a big patch of mange on his face went away. "The bull looks good now," Namgay said.

"It's the peaches."

"I think the cowboy got medicine from the vet."

"Well, he might have gotten medicine, but I think the peaches helped more."

"It doesn't matter," Namgay said. "He's better."

Namgay has a way of cutting through my clutter.

Sometimes I feel sad for the racehorse that couldn't live in the mountains. I look at my garden every day and pine for the chaotic color it once had, but I love my friend Pema more. He makes me understand that our hearts contain our greatest strength. I'll probably never stop trying to tame the bull. I know who I am. I'm not perfect. But it's really okay.

Acceptance is so much a part of being happy. First of all, accept who you are in all of your misshapen glory; and then, accepting others is a piece of cake. Mmmm, cake.

LAUGH IN THE
FACE OF DEATH

The Bhutanese make good use of humor. They use it for teaching and self-correction, and even discipline can be thinly disguised as humor in Bhutan. It's easy to laugh here, because things seem more relaxed and everybody is inclined in that direction. There's a lot of self-awareness as a result. It's tied to humility and subjugation of ego, and these are Buddhist attributes as well as part of the national character. Look at their patron saint, Drukpa Kuenley, the 17th-century holy man whose humor was a big part of his teaching. His stories are raw and raucous and involve fire shooting out of his penis to subdue demons (those who opposed the faith), and a lot of inappropriate behavior with farm wives. Granted, he's not everyone's cup of tea. He was 50 shades of gray before anyone knew there were more than a couple of shades. Most every village has a "joker," and *atsaras*, naughty clowns, who are important parts of teachings at *tsechus* (festivals).

Being able to laugh at yourself, having healthy humility, boosts your self-esteem as well as your immune system. It is the ultimate act of self-confidence. I'm laughing at myself right now because I'm trying to write seriously about not taking yourself seriously. Learning to laugh, and not just at funny movies or videos of cats falling off kitchen countertops or scaring themselves in the mirror, or jokes, or other people, but at yourself in all of your humanness and frailty, is about embracing humility and discarding egotism. Humor is a force of nature, an act of supreme will, a precious commodity. Every day there is too little of it in the world and when we have a chance to be serious or be humorous, I say be a clown and leave them laughing. If you're going to fall on your ass, then make a splash. Be sure there's someone watching.

The world is an absurd place. There's also a lot that's not funny, that certainly shouldn't be laughed at, like abuse, climate change, trafficking, hunger, war, imperialism, French manicures, and a whole host of horrible things. But those aren't the issues I'm addressing now. On a very basic, day-to-day level, life is, well, pretty funny. Clothes crack me up, especially clothes in Bhutan because I wasn't made for any of the fashions the small, slender Bhutanese women wear. Yet I am forced by circumstances to embrace my sartorial lot. I've been to ceremonies where my Bhutanese kira, the floor-length dress of Bhutanese women, decides of its own volition to deconstruct, and all the safety pins holding it together opt to pop out all at once. I've tripped numerous times on the tail of my kira— and if you wear it right, a kira doesn't actually have a tail.

Being the "other" in a society is certainly useful for honing my sense of humor, and most of all it helps me manifest humility, if by manifesting humility you mean shucking and jiving in the face of adversity. You can stick it or you can schtick it, and I for one prefer the latter. I know suggesting you make yourself foolish in your own eyes as well as others' might seem like a weird thing, but in truth it is profound. Humor helps us cope with a lot of uncertainties and vagaries and difficulties that all of us face, no matter where we are. Travel comes to mind. I know it's a tired cliché, but there's nothing more universal than a smile—try it when you're getting hassled by an Indian airport security worker. It's the last thing he or she expects and it will confuse them. He's spotted you as a Westerner and probably an American, and he desperately wants to go to the U.S. and make a lot of money, which he assumes you have. Anyway, he's not going anytime soon—probably not in this lifetime—and you are. So he's pissed. And bored. And filled with ennui. And he has a little power over you and your carry-on. And you are so easily perturbed, you Americans. You're hotheads. You're like cats getting poked with sticks, easily agitated, and it takes you a long time to calm down. Besides, you are arrogant. You must be put in your place.

When the Indian official asks you to step aside into the little holding area and open your suitcase, instead of seizing up and contorting your face and heaving sighs and doing all that whacked-out body language, smile like a bemused Buddha. Maybe you are arrogant and agitated and worried about missing your flight. Don't act like it. Keep smiling. But not maniacally. Just bemusedly or contentedly. Do everything he says with that inscrutable Buddha smile, and he will let you go, after he's poked around a little in your stuff—I guarantee it. That is, unless you have something illegal in your bags. Or batteries. He'll want to take the batteries.

Actually if you do this enough, just smile and cope when things are going wrong, especially when you're out of your element, like when you're traveling, then you'll actually start to feel it. Things will get better. That smile will protect you when the Indian airport worker is confiscating your batteries. And maybe you can even laugh when you get back home and tell the story.

Laughing in the face of adversity goes hand in hand with kindness. It's the ultimate kindness, really, because it's a way to be kind to yourself. It's a way to calm yourself down, and it helps defuse a situation. And if you're laughing you're not lashing out at others. I think of it as a way to get between myself and my ego and acknowledge the incongruity that, if you really think about it, permeates everything.

If you can embrace the absurdity that is all around us, you will be so much happier and prettier, and kinder, and your teeth will be straighter. Once, in Thimphu, Namgay had asked me to get a few art supplies for him. He wanted tracing paper, so I went to my favorite stationery store and asked the saleswoman if they had any.

"No, Madam."

"Oh. Okay. I thought you had some . . . could have sworn you had . . . wait! What's that in the corner? In the tube. Leaning up against the wall."

"That big tube?"

"Yes."

"It is tracing paper, Madam."

"Wait . . . I thought you said . . . Oh, well, never mind . . . May I buy it?"

"No, Madam."

"Why not?"

"It is twelve hundred ngultrum, Madam."

"Well, yes, that's a lot of money, isn't it? Nonetheless, I would like to buy it. May I buy it?"

"Yes, Madam."

That is a faithful transcription of what actually went down. I even borrowed a pen and a sheet of paper before I bought the tracing paper so I wouldn't forget. I don't know why the saleswoman said there was no tracing paper. Maybe she assumed I didn't want to buy a whole, enormous roll of it a mile long. Maybe she assumed that since it was a little pricey I wouldn't want it. She was acting as a sort of agent of fiscal responsibility. Maybe she forgot she had it. Maybe she was too lazy to think about doing a transaction. I have no idea, really. But this kind of absurdist thing happens a lot in Bhutan. You can get upset or you can laugh. It's your choice.

If you learn to laugh at little things then you'll be better prepared to cope with bigger things. In August 2005 my mother called me from Nashville and asked me to come home. I'd lived in Bhutan for eight years and she'd never asked me to come home. She'd never asked me to do anything. But she was dying. I said of course, but I said it could take me upwards of a week to make my travel arrangements and travel from Paro, Bhutan, to Bangkok, Thailand, then Tokyo, Detroit, and Nashville. I'd have to organize and coordinate plane tickets and arrange a hotel for the layover in Bangkok. It's not easy or fast to get anywhere from Bhutan. And at the time there was no way to make the arrangements online like there is now. Every flight required a ticket in hand and payment in cash. The logistics were especially hard with short notice as it was high tourist season and every Southeast Asian who wasn't nailed down was on his or her way to Bangkok for a vacation.

Of course I didn't mention any of this to her. I only said I'd come as soon as I could. "I'll wait," she said ominously.

The truth is I wasn't terribly close to my mom. We were just different people. I moved halfway around the world. She liked to stay home. I loved books. I never saw her touch a book. But she was beautiful and kind and she liked my sense of humor. And I liked to make her laugh. The cancer she'd been struggling with for almost seven years was finally taking over and she wanted me in her corner.

She didn't want a lot of fuss or weeping or drama, she said. She asked me not to let people stand over her and cry. She'd be at home with help from hospice. If I could have put on a clown suit and bounded into the room or ridden in on a tiny bicycle or jumped through a flaming hoop, I would have. I was ready to help her move on.

Namgay drove me to the airport in Paro and we sat in the car in sad silence, me thinking of the arduous trip I had in front of me, and of Mom. I had four days, and a travel gauntlet that included taxi rides, bus rides, hotel rooms, five plane rides, and six cities until I made it home. Namgay carried my suitcase into the airport, set it down, and we stood there for a minute or so holding each other, me clinging to him and he to me. We'd never been apart since we'd married. He kissed me and said good-bye. I turned to walk away and heard him call out, "Wait!"

I turned around and looked at him, expecting him to say something that fit the gravity and romance of the situation.

"Bring Neosporin!" he said, an urgent look on his face.

I burst out laughing. "Okay," I said, and kissed him again.

I got to Nashville, and, like any good Southern woman when there's an imminent death, I started cooking. Mom could drink water and coffee and juice, but she couldn't eat. "You can live over a month on liquids," I said. "I read that somewhere." She smiled. She knew I was bargaining for her.

Every day she lost a little of that vitality, that life force, and after about ten days I could see she was having a tough time. Her body was dying, although she never once complained of pain or discomfort. The best thing was to sit on the bed as she lay there and go through old pictures with her. She couldn't do it for long. She'd get confused and too tired.

She told me to get people out of the room if they came to see her and got weepy. She was very strong about what she wanted and what she didn't. She was dying on her own terms. She talked with her minister and my father and they organized her memorial service, the music, the Bible verses, every detail. She even asked me to show her what I was going to wear at her memorial service. I did, but I felt shy about it. "It's okay," she said.

I was living to help her die. I hoped it wouldn't be long. I put all of my energy into being cheerful and upbeat and making inappropriate jokes. My mother loved them. I helped her brush her teeth; she couldn't make it to the bathroom anymore so I held a crescent-shaped stainless steel emesis bowl supplied by the hospital at her mouth and brushed her teeth for her. She liked it because I called it her "drool bucket."

The hospice people gave lots of reading material and advice. One morning when the nurse came, I walked outside with her after she told me that my mother's pulse was almost nonexistent. "It won't be long now. Encourage her to take the morphine if she wants it," the hospice nurse said. "It will make it easier. She doesn't need to feel any pain. When she takes it, she'll go to sleep. And she probably won't be conscious anymore."

I was relieved, horrified, scared, sad, and angry. I was losing Mom. The next afternoon I asked her if she was in pain. "No," she said. And then a few seconds later she said, "Uncomfortable."

I didn't say anything, and then she said, "Do you think I should take the morphine?"

"I absolutely think you should take the morphine," I said in the most even, nonchalant tone I could muster. Inside I was alarmed. I wanted to scream, *NO! Hell no, I don't think you should take the morphine. That means you're checking out!* But I said yes. She wouldn't have asked my advice if she hadn't wanted to take the drug. She needed to feel that it was okay.

So she took it. I sat with her and took her hand and looked at it. It was still beautiful. My mother's hand. I was wondering when she would go to sleep. The hospice nurse said she'd go to the next stage, into a deep sleep. We didn't speak.

After a moment my mother whispered, "Linda?"

"Yes?" I jumped up and got close to her face so she could see me. "Yes," I said again.

"Would you do something for me?"

"Anything."

"Would you go in the bathroom and get my mirror and tweezers?" She put her hand up to her chin. "And get this hair."

"What?"

"It's bothering me."

"Mom?" I couldn't help myself. I started to giggle. "Mom . . ." I said again. And then I started laughing uncontrollably. She was too weak to laugh much but she smiled faintly and let out a little burst of air. "You want me to tweeze a hair on your chin? Now?"

"I meant to do it earlier."

That sent me into a fresh fit of laughter. "So much for grand gestures!" I said. But of course I did it. I held the mirror while she felt her chin. "Here," she said. It was a coarse gray hair, almost invisible. I tweezed it out gently.

I was still giggling. "You are something else," I said. I looked over and she had closed her eyes. I so love that memory of her last request and that we had a last laugh. She was a beautiful woman, fastidious in her appearance, and to the very end she was well-groomed. I think of it now and smile, and then I laugh and I cry at the same time.

Chapter
9

GENEROSITY
IS CONTAGIOUS

In Buddhism there are beings on the earth called bodhisattvas, enlightened humans who walk around among us. They have chosen to stay on earth and help other sentient beings attain enlightenment, instead of transcending to the heavenly realms. They are the ultimate pay-it-forwarders.

The Bhutanese share food, clothing, shelter, cars, time, ideas, laughter, money, jokes—just about anything—with friends, family, and complete strangers. It nearly makes my head explode how little they have and how easily they can let go of it. They like stuff as much as the rest of us. But they have a natural propensity to give, and it's not tied to how much they have, like tithing where you give a certain percent of your income to the church, or giving to a charity that's a 501(c)(3). It's like nothing else I have ever experienced.

In Bhutan I've learned that giving creates its own abundance. Things like food and clothing and even cars get distributed evenly, magically, miraculously, somehow. When people are generous, there always seems to be enough. People who visit Bhutan remark that although it's a poor country, nobody looks destitute.

Most who are munificent in Bhutan are hardly wealthy. The lowliest sustenance farmer will treat you like a king or queen if you visit his house. I'll never forget a beautiful pair of gold and silver *koma*, the large brooches that hold the sides of a kira together, given to me by a little girl whose father was my driver many years ago. "She wanted you to have something to remember her," her father told me as he pressed them into my hands. I tried to refuse them, but it was no use.

As in many traditional societies, giving bestows importance on the giver. It's always better to give than to receive.

As much as I admire this generosity, old habits die hard. A few months after Namgay and I married, we moved to a farm in Lungtenphu just outside Thimphu. One day there was a knock at the front door. As I went to open it, I heard people chanting prayers. There were two young, gawky Bhutanese men standing there with big cloth sacks. They wore ancient, dusty *ghos* (the traditional Bhutanese men's dress) and flip-flops. I smiled. They kept chanting. I smiled more. They chanted more. "You have the wrong house," I said, my teeth still clenched in a smile. I thought they might have come to perform in someone's household religious ceremony that the Bhutanese perform annually. One shook his sack and then made a gesture with his hand to his mouth.

Namgay came up behind me and greeted them.

"What do they want?" I said.

"They want rice."

"You're kidding! What for?"

"For the usual reason," he said, laughing.

"I know, to eat. But they're begging!" I said trying to sound as indignant and self-righteous as I possibly could, my eyeballs boring my patented electronic-beams-of-disapproval holes into them. Even if they couldn't speak English they'd certainly catch my tone and my crazy eyes. "I thought begging is against the law in Bhutan."

Namgay didn't answer. He was busy going to the kitchen and bringing back a bowl full of rice. He dumped a little into each of the young men's sacks.

I continued registering my starchy disapproval. "Look at them! Why are they going door to door begging? They're young and strong. Why don't they work? Why don't they get jobs?"

"This is their job," said Namgay, being annoyingly agreeable. He nodded to the men and smiled. They smiled back, bowed, and, resuming their chants, turned to leave.

True, the young men were probably farmers and they'd probably eaten their store of rice for the year. Maybe wild boars ate their family's supply of corn. Maybe there was a drought. They probably weren't slackers. And it's not like they could apply for grants or have a yard sale or bake sale or do Kickstarter. Even still.

"I don't mind giving to people, but I don't like them to ask me or beg me for things," I said to Namgay. "I like to give of my own volition." *Volition?* Why was I sounding so pompous and dragon-y? Even I wasn't buying it.

"The people who ask, the people who may not even need it and ask you for something, are the people you have to give to. People who are ungrateful and who don't thank you," Namgay said, "if you can give to these people, then you are a bodhisattva."

"That's right, play the bodhisattva card," I said.

A few days later I went to the weekend vegetable market to look for eggs. I couldn't find any for sale and when I walked out of the pavilion I saw an old man with wild white hair. He was missing some teeth and had his leathery hands pressed together as if to pray. He stood shaking them in greeting to people as they walked by. As I moved past him he pointed to something on my coat. I'm a bit of a magnet for crazies or drunks, but he didn't really look to be either. It was winter, on a sunny and cloudless day, but cold enough to see your breath. The old man was less than five feet tall and he had a short white beard—a little gnome in a worn gray gho and old Chinese army boots, with no socks. His legs looked cold.

I looked down at my coat, but there was nothing there. He gestured again and said something in a dialect I couldn't understand. I asked a passing boy what the old man said. They had a long conversation. I mean, it went on for 20 minutes, and then when I asked the boy what the old man said, he said:

"He wants a coat like yours."

That was it. A one-sentence explanation. How very Bhutanese.

"I got it at Palden's Shop," I said, happy to be of service and quite pleased that my new quilted, navy blue, thigh-length jacket was getting some attention, even if it was from an old village man who looked like an eccentric garden gnome.

The boy and man had yet another 12-hour exchange. This time there was pointing and broad hand gestures.

Finally the boy said, "He says he doesn't know where that shop is."

I was going in that direction, so I told the boy to tell the old man I could take him to the shop. I gestured for the man to follow. He smiled broadly and we set off. We must have been an unusual couple when, ten minutes later, we stood together in the middle of Palden's, which was filled with weekend customers, mothers and fathers with their kids. Palden's has been my favorite clothing store for many years. It has factory seconds and overruns of all kinds of clothing made in the factories of Bangladesh. The owner of the shop buys bundles of the clothes and pays by weight. He brings them to his shop and distributes them in big cardboard boxes lined up in rows on the floor. You can find cheap serviceable clothes in Thimphu if you don't mind digging through the boxes. Some of the clothes are hung on makeshift racks, but I actually like digging in the boxes. When shopping for clothes in Thimphu it helps if you're not picky about size or color—or style, or age, or level of cleanliness of the garments. And if you're flexible about gender it also helps.

I started digging in the boxes looking for a coat like mine, which I'd bought a couple of weeks before. It was navy blue, quilted, with silver snaps, lightweight but very warm and close fitting. It was the perfect coat. My favorite feature was the two big pockets, waist level in the front with Velcro on the flaps. The old man stood looking a little helpless and out of place, like he'd lost the toadstool he lived under. I could tell he was shy to be there, had probably never even been in a shop in Thimphu, and had probably come from a remote village. *He must have come to buy a coat,* I thought. Maybe he came on the bus, or got a ride in a truck. He might have relatives in Thimphu. I wondered where they were. The other customers ignored the old man for the most part, but I could see some of them cutting glances at him and me as they shopped.

He didn't seem to speak any Dzongkha or English or Spanish or German, which are the four languages I know, and I had no idea what dialect or possibly separate language he was speaking, so I started talking in English and relied on tone and gestures. I had an armful of coats I'd dug out of the boxes and I held one up. No. He shook his head. He didn't like it. I tried another. Yes. He liked it. I helped him put it on and the sleeves nearly dragged on the ground they were so long. "Oh! Hahaha!" we laughed. I was starting to have fun. It was a village man makeover!

I noticed that our fellow shoppers, instead of discreetly eyeing, were now overtly staring at us and paying close attention to our shopping expedition. I'm an exhibitionist out of habit in Bhutan. I can't help myself. Anywhere I go people will stare at me. Not because I'm remarkable to look at, or extraordinarily turned out (although I try my absolute best), but because even after many years, I'm still a foreigner, an anomaly, a friendly Southern American woman who looks like she might at any time do something outrageous.

Also I am a frustrated stylist. You can ask any of my friends. When they need a wedding dress, a suitcase, a pair of eyeglasses, boots, an outfit to make their ex-boyfriend jealous, a pair of jeans, or a pair of sneakers, I'm the first person many of them call. I have a friend who swears her husband proposed to her because she wore a hot-pink dress I picked out for her. I, in turn, get a contact high from helping other people shop for fun things, and then not having to pay for them. So it was probably divine providence that the old village man found me.

We finally found a nice, warm quilted coat similar to the one I was wearing.

"Just so you'll know," I said, helping him on with the coat, knowing he couldn't understand, "a ladies' petite extra large is a very good fit for you. And you can wear just about anything Jones New York. You totally own it."

I showed him how to use the snaps to close the coat. And Jesus Christ in the foothills, did he ever love the snaps! *Snap. Unsnap. Snap. Unsnap.* Snaps are genius, really, and so much better than buttons, especially for elderly fingers that have spent a lifetime farming. For fun I grabbed the coat at the bottom and jerked it and the snaps popped open with a satisfying *POP, POP, POP.* He laughed gaily. I led him to a full-length mirror so he could admire himself, and he ran his dirty hands down the front of the coat lovingly, lingeringly, as if he couldn't believe it was real.

"You want?" I asked in English. "*Go ne?*" I asked in Dzongkha. He smiled shyly.

Since we were there, I thought we should probably get him some socks. I looked around and found two thick, black pairs of kneesocks in one of the boxes.

"Get these, too," I said. "They'll hold up nicely." I pantomimed with one of the socks for him to put them on. He had a seat on a wooden stool in the corner and took an extravagant amount of time taking off his shoes, wiping the bottoms of his feet, and putting on the socks. His bare feet were reminiscent of hooves. We found some nice fleece track pants in a big box of children's clothing, and a warm red sweater to wear under his gho.

"I think we're done here," I said, taking the clothes in my arm and making my way to the front of the store where the owner, Mr. Palden, always sat behind a little desk near the door. "How much is all of this?" I asked, handing him the clothing. "He's wearing a pair of socks," I added.

Mr. Palden said it was 1,200 ngultrum, the equivalent of about $25. I held out my hand to the old man, hoping he would understand that he needed to pay.

Mr. Palden looked at me incredulously. "He doesn't have any money," he said.

"Oh," I said in a small voice. "Of course not." I hadn't thought of that. And then it was clear. But the boy had said . . . Oh. I felt stupid. I was embarrassed. Well, never mind. Clearly I had to buy these clothes, except I didn't have enough money with me. And Palden's Shop was one of the few places in Thimphu where you couldn't buy now and pay later. Mr. Palden always insisted on cash. And no discounts.

"You know me," I began sweetly. "I've shopped here so many years. May I bring you the money tomorrow? Please?"

Everyone in the store had turned to watch the drama.

Thankfully, Mr. Palden said yes, I could bring the money tomorrow, and he rolled the extra socks and pants and sweater in some newspaper, making a tight little package. The old man wanted to wear the coat, of course. Mr. Palden handed the man his parcel, and as I turned to walk out, a very sweet, very wonderful thing happened. Out of the corner of my eye I saw a discreet hand slide a little wad of money toward Mr. Palden on the desk. And then someone else put another bill with it, and someone else added more.

I turned around and men and women were fishing for money in their handbags, pockets, and *hem chus*—the big pockets made by the folds in the front of their ghos and kiras.

"Enough!" cried Mr. Palden. "It's enough!" he said, laughing and gathering the bills. I stood frozen at the door with my mouth open.

"Go!" he said to me, waving his hand toward the door.

"*Cadenche*. Thank you," I mouthed to the assembled shoppers, but no sound came out. I had a huge lump in my throat.

To celebrate I took the old village man and his new community-procured wardrobe to a Nepali canteen and bought us a plate full of hot samosas with lots of ketchup and hot sauce and some tea with milk and sugar. We sat across from each other at a booth, eating quietly and contentedly. I thought about the day.

As a whole the Bhutanese are the most generous people I've ever met. This was a few years ago and Bhutan is changing, but even now Bhutanese people are hardwired to be generous, and they still help each other in both small and big ways.

Many residents of Thimphu remember the "mad monk" who roamed the streets for years in rich, red, flowing robes carrying an ancient silver teakettle. Everyone knew him. He was harmless, slightly wild-eyed, and reputed to be the reincarnation of a high lama. He charged around the city with long, iron-gray hair, a beard, and an energetic stride, although he probably had nowhere particular to go.

Like many people with mental disorders, he had an aversion to being inside, and his family had given up trying to contain him. There were no drugs or hospital facilities for someone like him. He kept running away from the family home, to stomp and stride around the streets of Thimphu. People made sure he was fed and clothed and every once in a while someone cut his hair and gave him a bath. He slept on a concrete slab just off the main road. We'd see him there at night, under a big pile of blankets donated anonymously under cover of darkness by towns-people. Late one fall, when the weather started changing and the nights had gotten colder, some compassionate soul built a wooden frame around his concrete sleeping slab and stretched heavy plastic over the four walls and top to keep the wind out. There was even a little door with hinges! Soon the little plastic house was filled with more blankets. The monk could be a little warmer yet still feel unencumbered, and if he woke up in the night he could look up and see the stars. No one ever came forward to admit to building the little hut. But why would they? It's Bhutan.

You'll never outmaneuver a Bhutanese in largesse. They understand that generosity and kindness make a society. Nothing more. It's so simple.

If you do something nice for somebody you actually get more karmic points if you keep it to yourself. So I can tell you that now I do take opportunities to be kind here and there, but I won't say too much more than that. And I'll graciously give a cup of rice to a down-and-out farmer if he or she shows up at the door.

Chapter
10

WALK IN SACRED PLACES

I live to walk in the mountains of Bhutan.

People who traversed these mountains wrote the history of the country. They describe miraculous events as well as migration—more than you might think given the difficulties of getting around. The people and animals traveling through the Himalayas—traders, holy men and women, yogis, yoginis, soldiers, spies, scoundrels, and adventurers—wore ancient paths crisscrossing the highest corners of the world. I like to think it was because they were addicted to the immense beauty and the way walking in the mountains changes the scale of things and makes you feel like part of something bigger and profound.

Your soul feels like it's part of the landscape when you're walking around here. It's the closest I come to feeling religious. Perhaps it's because walking in the remote mountains, or anywhere for that matter, slows me down mentally and diminishes the volume of my inner voice, putting me in a meditative frame of mind. You have to get from point A to point B, and there's nothing else to do but enjoy and relax in that feeling of suspension. Nature gets in to your body. Thoughts and time, if you walk long enough, disappear, and you are only putting one foot in front of the other, following a path. There is a sense you have always been walking. You will always be walking.

Self-propulsion is the greatest thing in the world. It gives merit, humility, and power. Long ago, before political boundaries and nation-states, when just running into a stranger walking about in these mountains was something close to a miracle, stories seemed to travel on the wind. One of my favorites is the story of Ani Palmo.

Ani Palmo was the daughter of a king in ancient Bhutan who, against her father's wishes, became a Buddhist nun, a devotee of Chenrezig, the Compassion Buddha. She lived in a nunnery high in the mountains until she had the bad luck to catch leprosy and was kicked out. Hey, it wasn't all roses in the nunneries, folks. All alone, save for a devoted attendant, she tried to make a pilgrimage to a Chenrezig temple somewhere in Eastern Bhutan. On the way her body failed her. I imagine bits and pieces falling off. She collapsed and prepared to die. Then, the story goes, the temple turned around and came to her.

Religious texts are full of pilgrimages, raids, visions, and natural phenomena, and there are a handful of more prosaic British accounts starting with diplomat George Bogle's journal of his visit in 1774, which went rather well. Others, not so much. Some of the Brits' descriptions of traveling through Bhutan on the way to Tibet, or to try to get the Bhutanese to stop making raids into the Duars (the river valleys and plains of India) and sign treaties, are unintentionally hilarious. Anthony Eden, for example, makes no effort to hide his epic disdain for his hosts, and the Bhutanese make no effort to be helpful or be anything but ineffectual and dull. You can see as things devolve in Eden's journal. They were uninvited guests, after all, and wore their arrogance and haughtiness like crisp uniforms. You can also see how the Bhutanese, led by the larger-than-life Jigme Namgyel, the Black Regent, just fixed them right up by introducing them to local "customs" like taking a big swig of cow's milk and spitting it in their guests' faces. The Brits write about trudging through 40 inches of snow on a pass, or enduring 20-hour marches through the worst possible landscapes of nettle-filled, vermin-infested, cliff-hanging trails and raging rivers. Could it be the Bhutanese didn't suggest the most direct, least dangerous routes? There are good reasons they were never colonized.

What I love is that in Bhutan it's immaterial whether stories are mythical or real. And what is real, anyway? Certainly not the "reality" we see on American television. But I digress. At 17,000 feet in the Himalayan foothills all bets are off as far as what's real and what isn't. I'm not a doctor, but I know that there are three very important things that happen physiologically and mentally to your body when you spend time up in the mountains: you develop a high threshold for pain, your memory goes away, and I forgot the third thing. That's an old mountain climber's joke.

Large swaths of your brain cells may die when deprived of oxygen, but I hope they might be replaced by something else. I'm sure the oxygen or lack thereof was conducive to visions and helped blur the line between myth and reality as the ancients were recording what they saw and did. I'm of the mind that in an organic way, anything we ingest, including air, alters our reality. Seeing and remembering has to be influenced by the state of becoming that walking creates, and the mind and body working together. Walking in the mountains reminds me of the name of one of my favorite books, Lawrence Weschler's *Seeing Is Forgetting the Name of the Thing One Sees*, which comes from a quote attributed to Valéry.

But never mind the *mental* toll of wandering in the mountains. It is grueling, violent exercise. Many wanderers simply wore their bodies out. But there are tricks. Once someone really smart, my friend and stalwart walking companion Marie Brown, told me how to "swarm" up a hill to conserve strength. Instead of walking purposefully in a straight line, I put one foot in front of the other, focusing on the area just above the ground in front of me, encompassing that 180-degree arc in my line of vision. I try to be aware of all of my senses—sight, smell, touch, taste, and hearing—as much as I can. *What am I smelling? What can I hear? What do I see?* and so on. It really gets me operating at my peak ability. Then I visualize splitting up in a hundred thousand pieces, like a swarm of bees. I don't concentrate so much on walking a straight line from one place to the other, but rather on lifting one foot and then the other foot to that point just above the ground somewhere in that arc in front of me. I move forward but not purposefully, and not in a straight line. At the end of the day when my legs are aching and I'm bleary, I do this to go up a hill. Trust me. It's much easier to let your mind do most of the work.

Your sense of time and space and your vision and your sight and your sense of touch—everything changes walking in the mountains. Life is measured not by time, because time stretches, but by place. Each step moving yourself over the landscape reveals the organic connection between this Buddhism in Bhutan and how it meshes with the natural world. It's spiritual, but not religious, a tangling of body and mind. If your mind and body aren't working together, then you simply won't make it.

It does something to me I can't quite put my finger on; maybe it is the thin atmosphere and oxygen deprivation. Above the tree line, sounds disappear and that changes one's perception. There is no place quieter on earth. You might as well be on the moon. You can "hear" the silence reverberating. And as you watch a herd of Himalayan blue sheep in the distance migrate silently across impossible precipices you might see one dislodge a boulder as he leaps off it. You see the rock like a white speck tumble down the blue mountain, but you hear the faint cracking maybe five seconds later. It brings to mind that old philosophical question about the falling tree. (If a tree falls in the forest and there's no one there to hear it, does it make a noise?)

Memory certainly gets a little fuzzy walking in the clouds. Maybe that's why the stories are so fantastic. You can see where the idea of pilgrimage, going somewhere for a spiritual purpose, came about. There was a lot of pilgrimage traffic on these old Himalayan routes as well as flight from hostile forces, or a desire for better food and more comfort. Who knows what propelled them. I think people were wandering around looking for miracles.

Aside from the mental acuity, walking up high in nature can kill you. I have deep gratitude for men and women I've traversed the mountains with on treks, and feel a kinship with them. Some of them have saved my ample ass a time or two. Coincidentally a man named Phuntsho has accompanied me on every trek I've ever made in Bhutan. He spent time in the Army, and he can cook, set up a camp, build a fire, collect wood, find water, tend to horses, pitch a tent, stay dry in the rain, keep your spirits up, retrieve forgotten backpacks, make you laugh when you want to curl up and die, and more. He makes me jump over waterfalls and persuades me to climb down rock faces with his good-natured coaxing. Or if that doesn't work, he offers me plums or tiny thumb-size bananas. And if fruit doesn't work, he pulls out the trump card: a bar of chocolate. Yes, I resemble a donkey sometimes.

I'll be ambling along the trail, following the curve of a slate cliff to my left and minding the abyss on the other side, rain pelting down. I'll stagger a bit, and out of nowhere he'll be there—between the proverbial rock and the hard place (or chasm). Or I'll be staring blankly at a noisy river with strategically placed stones, steeling myself to hop over them and not get carried off by the raging waters. He'll come and lead me over the rocks, holding my hand. Only he'll be hopping backwards, so I can lock onto his steely eyes for encouragement, and he'll be wearing flip-flops instead of nice boots, and, if it's raining, a red-and-white-checked plastic tablecloth like a jaunty cape, his weathered elastic face and black hair and eyes always moving and laughing. He must be near 70, but he has that look of a human who is fit and focused and living a good life—a balanced, happy life. I aspire to be like him.

I generally have a good appetite and have been known to eat recreationally, but I flat-out can't keep anything down at high altitude. It comes back up, which is dangerous. Phuntsho and the other Bhutanese eat enormous platefuls of chilies, cheese, and rice for breakfast, lunch, and dinner, and I can't even look in their direction when they're doing it. It makes me sick. But he understands finicky American stomachs at high altitude and is infinitely patient and resourceful. Mornings on treks I'll awake to breakfasts of spaghetti with marinara sauce, egg rolls, eggs, rice, tuna, chilies, toast, jam, butter, biscuits, tea, apples, nuts, peanut butter and crackers, and cereal. He is trying the throw-everything-against-the-wall-and-see-what-sticks method, to hit on anything I can digest. And this is the wilderness, mind you. He's cooking all this over a fire with a couple of assistants. I've often wondered why Phuntsho doesn't just push me off a cliff. No one would ever know it wasn't an accident.

Mornings are surreal at high altitude, above the tree line. A thick, pearl-gray fog obscures everything. You can see ghostly shapes close by, making muffled snorts: a herd of yak in the mist. You must look down to your feet at all times when walking, because you can see only inches in front of you until the fog lifts, and you must negotiate piles of yak poop, varying in size and degree of freshness, from knee-deep hot and steamy dung, to crusty flat disks. You haven't lived until you've stumbled and kneeled into a big pile of freshly created yak poop. Nobody will get near you for a very long time. It's hard to love yourself.

Living and walking in the wilderness is a meditation and a discipline. The mind and body work in sync. If they don't, then you are dead meat. Nature can be random and violent. One night on a trek near Gangtey, a leopard came down and killed one of the horses, ripping its neck open. We all heard it, and I shook violently, alone in my tent, listening for footsteps or paws or the breath of a cat nearby. But if the leopard came for me I would most certainly never hear him. Leopards are stealthy. I was terrified.

The assistants to the cooks and horsemen on treks are always young and make me feel old and wobbly because in addition to their jobs slogging, carrying, pitching tents, and being otherwise useful, they expend massive amounts of energy playing tricks on each other. Once on a trek, one of the horseman's helpers, the best of the tricksters, told me that the cook's assistant's nickname was Po Tashi, and I should call him that. But I knew "Po Tashi" was idiomatic Dzongkha for "dickhead."

"Wait! Isn't that *your* nickname? I hear everyone calling you that," I said, making the horseman's assistant laugh. And of course that was his name for the rest of the trek.

I find it wildly alluring to walk behind the horsemen and their horses and listen to them talk to the horses and watch their efficient movements and their oneness with their surroundings. The horseman Tan Dorji is built like a yeti. He's an incredibly powerful man with huge, sinewy calves and a rough black beard and broad shoulders. He knows every stone on the paths; he knows instinctively the geographical point at which the sun will rise or set over a mountaintop or tree line. He knows by smell and sight and feel when the rain will come, and where to look just after a rain when sudden sunlight makes prisms of the raindrops that have collected on the grass. He moves his horses over the mountains by calling to them, persuading with his own horse language that only they and he understand. He looks poor in a faded gho and torn green Chinese army sneakers, but he is a rich man by Bhutanese standards. When we camped at Shaba the second day of a trek to Jumolhari, he went out after dinner to round up his horses. They were tiny specks way up on the mountain where they'd gone, God knows why, to graze. He didn't come back. It rained all night and at breakfast in the kitchen tent the next morning we saw him walking toward us in the steady drizzle. He didn't seem to notice he was wet to the bone. Anyway, by midmorning the Himalayan sun had dried him, for the most part.

Namgay and I have this thing when one of us leaves the house. Whoever is leaving says, "What may I bring you?" It was born of necessity for milk or vegetables or something for the house, but it's evolved into a joke. We try to think of the most absurd thing we can ask for. Once when I was leaving for a trek to Simikot, an area south of Thimphu, I asked, and Namgay said, "Bring me the summer hair from a cow's ear." He uses animal hair to make his brushes for his thangka paintings, and this hair is particularly fine but stiff—good for painting fine lines.

We had a laugh. But then, kind of miraculously, midway on my trek I did encounter a cowherd and some cows in a mountain meadow. I asked the cowherd, in my imperfect Dzongkha, if he'd trim some hair from inside one of his cows' ears. I was thinking someone who had hung out with the cows for years just might be able to do this. He pulled out his big *kichu,* or knife, and pulled a short clump of hair on a cow's flank and shaved it off rather precisely with the sharp blade.

"*Me me me!*" (No no no!) I said. "The hair inside the ear." Of course, he looked at me like I was peculiar.

"I will have to bring it to you," he said. "You go."

I swarmed up the mountain and forgot about it.

Early that evening, we were all waiting for dinner, drinking tea around the fire.

"Madam has a guest," Po Tashi announced, and behind him, here came the cowherd with a little presentation: a glossy green leaf with a little toothpick he'd carved from wood. In it was a plug of curly brown cow's hair, presumably from its ear. I gave him two hundred ngultrum, about $5, and the rest of the night everyone debated whether or not I overpaid.

I'll never forget the expression on Namgay's face when I presented it to him. It was a triumphant moment for me. He actually used the hair to make brushes, and it made a lot of them.

I try to simulate that walking in the Himalayas experience anywhere, getting out and into the woods to hike around, or walking in a park or on a country road, or a city sidewalk. I can feel that sense of time slipping away walking down Fifth Avenue in New York, or following the Skytrain route in Sukhumvit in Bangkok, or wandering in the woods in Tennessee. My sense of myself and my legs is strong. That is, in itself, a sacred place to be. I will always find sacred places, and I will always be walking in them, following that path.

PARENT YOURSELF

In 2005, we took Kinlay, a six-year-old Bhutanese girl from Namgay's village, to live with us. I was about as prepared to parent a child as I was to land a wide-body jet in Istanbul. That is to say I was facing it cold, palms sweaty, ill-equipped, and with an enormous sense of dread that I would fail.

Slowly it dawned on me that as I learned to live with this new order in our house and with this new being I must feed, clothe, educate, and otherwise nurture, I had to be sure also to do all of that for myself. It's like the instructions they give you before you fly: put the oxygen mask on yourself before you put it on the child.

Any good parent, or in my case, any half-assed parent, understands the value added to parenthood is that you get better at parenting yourself. At least, you should.

Being a mom to a child from a wildly different culture and background meant I had to stay grounded. I had to get as smart as I could as fast as I could. Mistakes would be made. I would see to that. That old cliché, "Failure is the pillar of success," is true. But luckily we're all still here, and things are okay.

Kinlay was a little girl who needed help. She had to walk over six kilometers to school every day in her village, and it was too hard for her. In Bhutan it's not unusual for relatives or friends without children of their own and in good circumstances to raise other people's children if it's needed. It's a good system, and it's about doing what's best for the kids.

From the moment she arrived, we plunged in, and the clock speeded up and never slowed down. I was so used to doing what I wanted when I wanted, rolling out of bed whenever it suited me. No longer. I couldn't believe how fast the days went by when everything revolved around drop-off and pick-up from school. My friends said, "Welcome to our world."

I bought Kinlay a Barbie doll and lots of matching Gap and H&M outfits. I suppose I wanted to Americanize her, make her into someone I could relate to. I had many Barbies when I was young, and shops all over Thimphu had Chinese knockoff Barbies. It was a little desperate of me. She dutifully put the doll on the shelf in her room and never touched it again. She preferred an old telephone cord that she'd rigged into a jump rope, and her prized possession was a collection of smooth rocks she used for a jacks-like game called "fivestones" that she played with her friends before and after school. She also liked to beat up little boys.

Her reading and math skills weren't very good, and she was behind her peers in school, so I tried to work with her every day. Kinlay would have none of it. I reprimanded her. She resisted. Neither one of us had a clue about what to do. But some things were not negotiable. No matter how much she wanted to pull the cat's tail, she couldn't. She had to control herself. So while I was teaching her this, it occurred to me that I could also use some self-control. I didn't need to get so angry. I didn't need to control so much.

It isn't so much about the mistakes you make, but about what you do with them that's the point of the exercise. Learning from them is optimal, of course, and not making the same mistakes over and over is also good. I've never had anything in my life that so clearly benefited from trying, failing, and then trying again as motherhood. Luckily Bhutanese children, and possibly all children, are amazingly resilient.

There weren't any resources anywhere in Bhutan, so when I had a spare five minutes I used to search "adoption" on the Internet and read what I could. According to one website, many "late-life adoptees," children older than five, often had issues with nurturing, or lack thereof. A lot of them didn't get held much as babies. So this site suggested actually holding the children. Imagine that. I didn't have time to discern whether this was an issue with Kinlay, but one day when she refused to go inside and do her homework, I sat down in the wicker chair in the garden and asked her to come to me.

"Ca che be?" (Why?) she asked warily.

"So I can hold you like you're my little baby," I said. She threw down her jump rope and came and curled up in my arms.

We did that as a routine for years, until she went away to boarding school. And now I realize it probably amused her more than anything else—something weird and kind of interesting that her silly American mom asked her to do. I think it did a lot more for me. It conditioned me to hold a child and nurture a child and love a child. My child.

The main thing I was always afraid of in our household was that it would be two Bhutanese against one foreigner, and I was afraid that because I had zero urge to be a parent, I'd turn out to be a bad one.

When Kinlay was nine, Namgay and I would be coming and going from the U.S. for the next few years, and we enrolled her in a boarding school in India. It is common in Bhutan if you can swing it financially to send your child to some of the excellent boarding schools nearby in Kalimpong and Darjeeling. Kinlay liked the idea. Like many children, she did well if her days were tightly scheduled. We had almost a year to prepare for it, talk about it, and make plans. She spent her winter break from school with her nose in books. She loved *Charlotte's Web*, but we struggled over *James and the Giant Peach*. We wanted her to be ready academically and emotionally, so we talked a lot about how it would be, although none of us had a clue as to how it would be.

From our house in Thimphu it was a six-hour drive to the Indian border, then another six hours driving through India to Kalimpong in the state of West Bengal to Dr. Graham's Homes. The school is an institution in "The Hills," and many of Bhutan's leaders were educated there. She'd have some Bhutanese friends there. Driving down to the border, we passed only five other cars spaced about an hour apart. At Gedu, there was the usual thick fog, and we had to inch along the road until it lifted. Kinlay slept in the backseat.

The next part of the trip was peek-a-boo with India. We'd crawl around a curve in the winding road, and the mountain vista would give way to blue skies. There we would spot a glimpse of the flatlands we were headed for, the river deltas of the Indian Duars, shimmering brown in the distance. We rounded another curve in the road and the mountains would come back full force. At yet another switchback, India would appear again, looking a bit closer this time, and looking less like an abstract painting. I considered waking Kinlay so she could see, but decided to let her sleep.

I was trying not to think of the reason we were actually in the car.

As we got closer to the border everything became lush and green, the air thick and humid. We stopped for the night at a hotel and then met our Indian car and driver to make the second half of the trip, due west through North Indian tea plantations to Kalimpong in the Darjeeling District.

At Phuentsholing, the Bhutanese town on the border with India, it was already midday. There were the ubiquitous Maruti cars parked at odd angles on the sides of the streets, and others honking their way through town. Many Indians and Bhutanese were shopping. It was all a sort of prelude to the frenzy of India.

The next morning our driver came to collect us in his Range Rover for the drive to Kalimpong. We passed through the town and made the left turn at the Bhutan Gate to the Jaigaon road and into uncontrolled pandemonium: skinny Indians in bright clothes; filth on a massive scale; goats, cows, dogs, cars, poop, dust, noise, and wafting smells of spicy food, petrol, and incense; more noise; more animals. In short: India.

"How's it going?" I asked Kinlay.

"It's going fine," she said. But her eyes were wide. She'd never set foot out of Bhutan.

Our driver, a sullen man with black Adonis curls, looked like a young, brooding poet. He was a masterful driver through the flotsam and jetsam on the roads across tea plantations. I thought of the return trip without Kinlay and got a pain in my stomach.

Everyone was carrying large baskets filled with grass on their backs or on their heads. It was jute-harvesting season and many of the farmers were taking their products to market. The road was straight and wide and we went about 60 kilometers an hour, but there were deep potholes, and the occasional goat, or cart filled with jute, or man on a bicycle, or motorcycle or dog would come out of nowhere, so Adonis had to swerve and slam on the brakes to keep from having an accident.

Every resident of the Indian state of West Bengal seemed to have acquired a cart, filled it with jute, and then pulled it like a rickshaw or attached it to a bicycle and come to a nearby village market to sell it. There were giant coils of jute piled ten feet high in the rickety wooden carts, and many of them had young girls in colorful saris sitting on top of the piles. There were people everywhere. Adonis blasted the car horn.

Finally we reached the calm green Kalimpong hills. We had a wonderful few days with Kinlay and her maternal aunt and uncle who had retired to Kalimpong after government service. It was such a relief to know they would be nearby while Kinlay was at school.

Finally the day came and we drove to the school, and I kept going over in my mind how it would be to leave Kinlay with her housemother and nine other girls at her cottage on the grounds of the school. I would downplay the whole thing, I reminded myself. I would even laugh a little and remind her that it would be a hard adjustment at first, and she might be sad and lonely, but then everything would change and she would grow to love it. I would give her a big hug and kiss, say "See you soon" or "I'll see you later" or "Be good," and then . . . What? . . . Oh, yes, I'd walk away and duck behind a building and sob. Which is exactly what I did.

But back at the cottage, amidst a crowd of parents and students, from my vantage point around the corner of a nearby building, I could see and hear Kinlay's elderly aunt begin to wail and reach her hands to the sky like a madwoman. Then she grabbed Kinlay and began rocking back and forth, stroking her hair and her face, and wailing and calling out words in another language I didn't know. It was quite a spectacle. After a moment Kinlay started to cry with her, and they had a good cry together, clinging to each other, still rocking back and forth.

I was furious. *How ridiculous! How mawkish! How dare she steal my thunder!* This woman lived in the same town as Kinlay. She would see Kinlay every Sunday! I had the impulse to run back to the cottage to have a do-over, but of course I didn't.

I remained sullen and angry, and I couldn't listen to my parent voice until we were almost to Thimphu. *Let it go. You can't control everything. Why, after living in this culture that is so different, are you still trying to control things?*

By then I was mostly mad at myself, and sad, and angry at the aunt. No need to be mad at myself, and no need to be angry with the aunt. She was probably feeling it, the separation. If not from Kinlay, then she was remembering her separations from her own children, or other separations from other loved ones. Who knows? The parent in me reminded the child in me that often I chose not to do something. I chose not to act because I didn't want to make a mistake or because it was too painful. I know that doing something, even if you make a mistake, is so much better than doing nothing. Whatever you do, don't be so hard on yourself.

Being a parent is great because it teaches you a new level of monitoring yourself. You are accountable in an infinite number of ways that people without children aren't. We all have deep and wide responsibilities to children. It is an unspoken oath that they come first, so it's better if you aren't self-absorbed. All of the qualities we want our kids to have—honesty, resilience, intelligence—we have to have in ourselves. We can't inspire these things in our kids if we don't have them.

Now, years later, when I'm in the U.S., I find I need to parent myself more than ever. I find that sometimes I'm so busy handling things, doing things, moving around, that I can't have proper emotions, or I won't allow natural emotions to come through, like I did or didn't do that day in Kalimpong. Sometimes my parental instinct kicks in, and I tell myself it's okay to be sad and lonely and miss things and make mistakes. It's the grand and glorious mess that is life. Kinlay is fine, by the way, and has grown into a teenager, albeit a Bhutanese one, which is a great accomplishment for all of us.

We all need that parent in us to tell us that conflict is okay, that emotion and following your heart is okay. We can all learn to note our various missteps, forgive, try to correct, and move on. And sometimes we need that parent to take us up in her arms and be sad with us, cry with us, and just be there.

YOU ARE
WHAT YOU EAT

Kinlay is the healthiest child I've ever known. She grew up in Bhutan with a trifecta of living in clean air, lots of walking, and good, whole, organic food. I've come to think of these things as our fundamental riches. In Bhutan you can eat a lot of good food and eschew the processed chips and snacks and frozen mystery meats that are sneaking into shops in Thimphu. Of course, people do eat them. And the office workers of Thimphu are figuring out that they can't eat their traditional diet of enormous quantities of rice, chilies, and cheese like Bhutanese farmers who work outside all day, or they'll get diabetes and heart disease.

Namgay and I still eat locally and seasonally for the most part. We stay active, and the nature of life here—the Buddhism, the culture, and the attitudes about work and play—is conducive to lower stress. We eat more whole foods, and cooking with friends or family is simply part of our day, every day. I've gone into offices around lunchtime and there's often a rice cooker boiling away on a table in the corner, and someone is chopping vegetables at his desk to help cook a communal lunch. Isn't that wonderful?

I'm not saying that everyone in Bhutan eats healthier than everyone in the U.S., but here it's easier to look at food differently. There's not as much of it. There's a lot of organic and unprocessed food. There's also some imported junk food, but the Bhutanese haven't yet reached the level of recreational eating that we have in the U.S. They make most of their meals from whole foods. I'm more holistic, more mindful, and less emotional about what I put in my mouth when I'm here. I know it's because there's just not nearly as much food around, and there's also not much variety. There's about one one-thousandth of things to eat as compared with the U.S. We eat about 10 or 12 things: rice, salad, soup, chicken, green beans, chilies, locally made cheese, carrots, oatmeal, coffee, tea, and whatever is in season, and that's about it. Food takes longer to procure and eat here; organizing meals is more deliberate, and therefore it's more integrated into everyday life. If you've planted and grown the food, harvested it, cooked it, and eaten it, you are in a serious relationship with it. You've expended time, emotion, and calories to get it.

I'm not saying that Bhutanese cuisine is particularly healthy, either. It's rice-based and full of chilies, cheese, and oil—carbohydrate-heavy fuel, great for going out and sowing paddy or doing other farm work, which is what most people do in Bhutan. So when they eat they eat for nourishment, not for noshing. It's not social so much as survival to eat as much as you can when you can, and then go outside and work like hell wrangling some yak.

There are a couple of restaurants with burgers and pizza in Thimphu, as well as coffee places with cakes, and bakeries, but you'd never say the words "fast" and "food" in the same sentence in Bhutan. You won't find a Starbucks, McDonald's, Wendy's, Subway, or Burger King. You can't stay in your car and get food.

For me, any thinking about food here begins and ends with the weekend vegetable market down by the river in Thimphu. I usually go on Friday afternoons after Kinlay is out of school so she can help carry the big woven baskets of tomatoes, onions, chilies, potatoes, cabbage, broccoli, carrots, and eggplant through the sprawling market. We handpick the produce, which is displayed in big bamboo baskets on the floors of each booth, and we can man-handle it, pinch it, smell it, and sometimes taste it before it gets weighed on ancient, handheld scales and then dumped in our baskets. We do this every week, and we get maybe 15 to 20 pounds of assorted spices, fruits, and vegetables, and maybe a few eggs and some cheese. We always visit the "Pineapple Guy," because he goes down to India and brings back amazing fruits and lets us sample. What's at the market depends on the season, and each season has its specialties.

During winter, sweet juicy oranges from the south flood the vegetable market, and the Bhutanese dry a lot of fruits and vegetables and eat plenty of dried pumpkin as well as *shakam*, little bits of dried beef we pressure-cook and add to curries. In the past, winter wasn't a good time for vegetables. We'd eat potatoes, cabbage, and dried chili—that was about it. Now, the farmers of Punakha are producing year-round broccoli, lettuce, carrots, beets, and many other vegetables.

Spring officially starts with asparagus and fiddlehead fern, which grow wild everywhere, as well as wild avocado, the size and shape of ping-pong balls with a nuttier, sharper flavor than avocados elsewhere. In summer the market is bursting with gorgeous vegetables, including the first crop of Bhutanese chilies, which are the national delicacy. Watch out if you see a big bowl of what looks like sliced green beans. It's probably very hot green chilies, so go easy if you're not used to intense heat. Summer also brings the new red rice. If you've ever eaten rice that's freshly harvested you'll understand that what we get in some American grocery stores like Whole Foods has been around for way too long, and a Bhutanese farmer would not eat it himself; he'd feed it to his livestock. August means corn and masses of peaches and hundreds of varieties of mushrooms, and in the fall, apples, pears, walnuts, and much more. It's the harvest time, after all.

All the vegetables we buy are organic, sold by vendors we've known for years. Many times we can see the actual fields where the crops grow, and we know the chickens whose eggs we eat. Once we went to see friends in Kabesa, just north of Thimphu, and we drove past a huge field of green beans on the way to their house. Namgay is fanatic about them, and he admired the rich green of the beans and remarked that they looked ready to eat. Sure enough, our friend's neighbor had brought a big sack to her that very day. We ate platefuls for dinner and they were wonderful.

In Bhutan there is no food marketing, no specials, no Whole Foods plexi-domes of cheese among the tomatoes. There's no cheese made by monks and aged in caves in France or produced in co-ops by dancing goats. Nothing has a fancy name. It's just "cheese," which is a cottage cheese from cow's milk, hand patted into balls that ladies sell out of buckets all over town, and "yak cheese," which comes in big slabs or in hard cubes called *chugo,* that you suck on. We eat Amul brand cheese from India, which is "American slices," or fake cheese, when real cheese isn't available.

We buy 50 kilograms of rice, which is over one hundred pounds, every three months and keep it in a big wooden rice box in the kitchen. We get nice bread, including bagels, from a Japanese bakery run by developmentally challenged Bhutanese near our house, and we get a little chicken and meat from the market.

In Bhutan there's integrity to the food because we are close to it and we see it being produced, and it's taught me that what we eat informs our character. There's an unfussiness that makes the food (and us) humble, and it's unpretentiously presented. You eat. You enjoy. You move on to something else.

To the average American it probably sounds boring. Living in Bhutan makes me realize just how difficult it is in the U.S. to eat healthy and well. And focus on quality as opposed to quantity. We don't realize the endless varieties of cookies, chips, cheeses, meats, breads, condiments, dips, and other gastronomic amusements that have advertisements on television, that pop up on our computer screens, on billboards, that come in the mail. Smells waft through shopping malls and airports. Food is absolutely everywhere. We are seriously and insidiously marketed to and food is designed (literally) to appeal to all of our senses. When you live in a place where you don't see cheese dripping off slabs of pizza and chocolate rivers flowing over cake and ice cream on television, and big, thick pieces of meat the size of your thigh delivered to your table on massive platters in restaurants, marinated, enhanced with flavor, drenched with barbeque sauce, and infused with color to be more appetizing, it changes your attitude. Food has less glamour and sex appeal in Bhutan. And in most places in the U.S., if you see something gooey and luscious on TV, all you have to do is pick up the phone and call and it will be delivered to your door. When you can't phone in an order, when you don't go to the store to find 20 new foods wrapped up in bright, colorful, attractive packages discounted and marketed to you, two for the price of one, right then and there, something remarkable happens: cravings go away. They really do.

In my life I have been something of a craving queen. As Americans we are taught that it's our right to satisfy our cravings. We're encouraged to do it. But I learned that if your taste buds and brain aren't in overdrive, continuously being overstimulated, confused, and marketed to, you can taste and enjoy the subtle deliciousness of simple, whole foods. Your brain and taste buds actually start paying attention to your stomach. Food is not such an emotional issue.

But like I say, I love ice cream and potato chips and all that stuff, so what I have to do when we're in the U.S. is try to simulate our eating lives in Bhutan. We limit what we eat to the same eight or ten things and rotate them every couple of weeks. We buy the same things at the grocery store every week, as if we're shopping in Bhutan. I have a mantra when I'm watching television: nothing tastes as good as it looks on the screen. We don't eat pizza unless we go to someone's house and they serve it, and we don't order takeout. I tell myself that some foods are off-limits: potato chips, Girl Scout cookies, peanuts, milk shakes, steak, donuts. Of course I slip off the rails occasionally. Once we were picking up a friend at the airport in

Nashville and the plane was delayed. We passed a Krispy Kreme donut shop on the way to the airport and we had some time, so I told Namgay he should try one. "You've never had a Krispy Kreme!" Of course I wanted him to have the experience, and of course I knew he would enjoy it more if I also ate a donut. We ordered two, ate them, and then he said, "That was good. I want another one." "Hmmm. Me, too," I said. Eight donuts later we called it quits. I don't know why but Namgay seems to be able to do something like that and keep his dignity and also not gain an ounce. I'm another story entirely. I had a very low moment the next morning when I woke up and went into the bathroom and had a look at myself in the mirror. There was a big dried blob of cream filling from the donuts stuck in my hair, which wasn't a good look for me. So. No more donuts.

I confess I am Southern to the core and sometimes after a year or two in Bhutan, eating in a very unassuming, very moderate and healthy way, I come to the U.S. and feel like a sailor on shore leave. I have periodic blackouts and wake up in the middle of the night on the floor surrounded by Kit Kat wrappers or chicken bones. Or worse, I pass out in my car and wake up in a parking lot somewhere with a half-empty bag of Cheetos in the backseat.

Eventually, instead of careening out of control, I take the reins of that buggy and get back on a simpler diet, because nothing tastes better than eating well. But I still eat fried chicken, and I even make it in Bhutan. Hey, I'm from Tennessee. It's practically required.

I wake up every morning to our cat calling for his breakfast at the back door. Namgay has already gotten up and is in the kitchen making tea. By the time I've washed my face and come downstairs, he's mixing yesterday's leftover rice with canned sardines for Man Cat, who got his name because he came around and Namgay called him "that man cat" for a while. When it was clear he was staying and had adopted us, we dropped the "that." We indulge him and honor him because he's had a hard life living in the woods of Bhutan. He's missing his tail and his left ear and is so beat-up and full of scar tissue he hardly looks like a cat anymore. He is not very cuddly. But he acts like a cat and has made it quite miraculously to old age. We weren't easily adopted, but then we succumbed, and after we all got comfortable, we provided him an opportunity to lose yet another part of himself and had him neutered.

Sometimes Namgay will mix some rice with the curry from the night before (curry is what the Bhutanese call any meat or vegetable in sauce you put over rice), and we have a little breakfast. Rice, with a dash of oil, and some salt, plus the curry, heated and stirred in a pan makes *toetse,* my favorite breakfast.

Preparing any meal in Bhutan starts with cooking rice, and Bhutanese red rice is preferred. It's hearty, nutty tasting, and is only grown on Himalayan slopes. When it's cooked, it turns a beautiful pink color.

You can't have a meal without chilies. In summer, they're grown in everyone's kitchen gardens. In wintertime, we eat dried chilies, which are festive and red and dried on tin roofs all over the country.

The national dish of Bhutan is *ema datse*—chilies and cheese. You can also add potatoes, mushrooms, meat, or other vegetables, but as long as it has a lot of chilies in it, it will be appreciated. To make ema datse, add a small bud of garlic, one-half cup of chopped tomato, and one-half cup of onion to a pan with an inch and a half of water in it. Namgay likes to add chopped ginger, but it's your call. Set the pan on the stove and heat it at medium high; add a tablespoon of oil (olive oil is good), and a dash of salt. Now add some chilies to the mix. In Bhutan we'd take four or five nicely washed chilies, cut off the tops, and quarter them lengthwise down the middle. Local chilies that are indigenous to Bhutan are preferred, but jalapeño chilies are a good substitute. You can also use those nice dried Mexican red chilies. The rule of thumb is if you think you have enough chilies, add a couple more. For less heat scrape out the seeds and toss them. Let the chilies sit on top of the garlic, tomatoes, and onions. Don't stir. Then crumble cheese on the top. Our homemade "cottage" cheese in Bhutan isn't homogenized and if it's a little rotten, then so much the better. If you don't have semi-rotten Bhutanese cheese hanging around, then goat cheese is a good substitute, or cow's cheese, or you can experiment with any cheese that will melt nicely. The pot will have been cooking for about five minutes by now, and you still haven't stirred anything. It's all just sitting there cooking into itself. Turn the heat to low, put the lid on it, and let it simmer for another 10 or 15 minutes.

Fluff up the rice you've cooked, dish some out onto a plate or into a bowl, turn off the stove, stir the ema datse, and dish some out onto the rice. It's a little bit masochistic, but a culinary experience like no other.

MOVE TO
THE MIDDLE
IN ALL THINGS

It's fly season in Bhutan. They come when the fruit appears on the trees, and leave in late summer after it's picked. They are a force to be reckoned with.

Once I was taking a walk down by the riverbank and heard a loud buzzing, like a chain saw, which is still a rarity in Bhutan, so I went to see what was up. I made my way through the trees and brush to an open field above the riverbank. A huge, black, living cloud of horseflies, about eight feet across, hovered over a newly delivered cow placenta.

I have come to think of the flies as reincarnated American lawyers, trying to fast-track their way back to humanity. Some of my best friends are American lawyers, but face it, they are easy targets. There aren't many lawyers in Bhutan; certainly not as many as there are flies. In 2006 a judge in Thimphu told me there were 67. This translates roughly to 1 lawyer per 10,000 people. There are probably more now, but there are still not many.

Justice is swift in the Bhutanese system, and often, for example, if two men are fighting in the streets of Thimphu and maybe there is a big crowd around them watching the fight, the police will come and put them both in jail. It doesn't matter who started it, or who was at fault.

Bhutanese law comes from no less than the Buddha himself, and also a man named Shabdrung Ngawang Namgyal, who unified Bhutan in the 17th century and did some codifying.

Now every Bhutanese citizen has access to the courts for mediation in settling disputes, divorces, accidents, and other legal issues. But most people, if they are unfortunate enough to have a problem, rely on mediation outside of court, an age-old, unwritten code of conduct to settle disputes.

Mediation has always been at the core of the Bhutanese legal system and now it has been written into the laws. Judges in Bhutan have to inform litigants twice during the course of a court case that they may stop the case at any time and mediate their dispute. Mediation has been used historically in the villages, where people don't have ready access to courts; they don't have a lot of money and need to settle disputes quickly and go on with their lives.

Once Namgay and I saw a mediation firsthand, near his village. Tashi, a Bhutanese woman, wanted to divorce her husband, Dorji. They had children and property. But the couple was of a certain age, their children were grown, and they were from a place where people didn't normally go to court to get a legal marriage. Back in the old days in Bhutan, and even now in many villages, there are no written marriage contracts. People just decide to live together as man and wife. Sometimes they just move in together. Sometimes there is a *puja,* or religious ceremony. If they have a little money there could be a party.

In the eyes of everyone but the courts, Dorji and Tashi were married and had been for many years, long enough to have grown children with families of their own. A mediator was called in, a headman from the village, to help dissolve the union, and both parties and their extended families agreed from the outset to abide by his decisions. This was important because many of the family members took part in the deliberation. They met each evening in Tashi and Dorji's house. Like any event in Bhutan where more than two people gather, there was a great deal of food involved and plenty of drink. Babies, children, and livestock were also a part of the proceedings. Everybody wanted in on the excitement because nothing much happens in the village that is of this level of interest.

Since there was still no electricity, and so no television, the mediation was a big event, sort of a home version of *Judge Judy.* In the kitchen women cooked meat and chilies over a mud stove. Others cut onions, garlic, and potatoes into big metal bowls, sitting cross-legged on the wooden floor of the kitchen. They kept up a steady stream of conversation punctuated with laughter.

"Ah! These men. They give so many problems."

"What is she thinking? She'll never be rid of him."

"Maybe their karma together is finished. Did you ever consider that?"

Outside, the men stood around a fire with a big pot of rice boiling over it. One man occasionally pulled the top off the pot and peeked inside. All speculated endlessly, raising points in the disputants' favor or remembering incidents that implicated one or the other.

"He's a big boozer. He loves his *chang*."

"We're all boozers. Does that mean our wives should divorce us?"

"Quiet! Don't give them any ideas!"

In the sitting room the mediation was more akin to a cordial chat among friends and family than a divorce proceeding. Tashi, Dorji, the mediator, assorted interested parties, and many children and babies congregated.

The elder listened as both sides presented their cases. He asked detailed questions. Someone brought him a fresh cup of tea. Tashi was very industrious and had a small kitchen garden. On less than half an acre of land she was able to grow enough carrots, potatoes, chilies, cabbage, tomatoes, and corn to feed her family. Plus she gave a little bit to her neighbors, and even had enough after that to sit at the road a few hours on Saturday mornings to sell her produce to passing cars. She sold eggs from her chickens and made cheese from her cow's milk. One of the big hotels in Thimphu sent a man once a week to pick up two rice sacks full of her fresh cheese. She was able to save a little money.

Dorji, who was not quite as industrious, routinely found where she hid the money, took it, and bought beer for himself and his friends. Years of this, as well as other petty and not-so-petty disputes between them had balled up into a large resentment, like a big cloud of angry flies.

In an effort to counter the wrongs and offenses of Tashi's claims, Dorji made his own inventory of her shortcomings: she nags him, she has a boyfriend, and her cooking is no good.

The alleged boyfriend was called in. No, he said, he had only been asked to repair the roof of her house. He came. He fixed the roof. She fed him. He left.

"What did she feed him?"

"She gave him pork and radishes with red rice."

"How is it she never cooked pork for me?"

"I never cooked pork for you because you are a pig yourself!"

"You see how it is for me!"

As negotiations went on it was clear the marriage was irretrievable. Both parties wanted out. This was obvious by the second night, and so for the remainder of the week the rights to properties owned by the couple were worked out.

It was her family's land and her family house they had lived in throughout their married lives, so there was no question that she would keep the house, the paddy, all the property she brought to the marriage. The Bhutanese system is matrilineal, so the women generally inherit property, and men, when they marry, move to their wives' houses.

As a way to appease him and get him out of her life, Tashi agreed, on the fifth night, to give him a lump sum of cash: the equivalent of about $160, her egg money for three months.

He took the money and went to live, briefly, at his sister's house in the next village over. After a few months he went to live with his daughter and her husband.

This is the way disputes are settled in the village, by talking it out among family and peers. That's not to say things don't get messy, or that things always go according to plan.

I wrote a version of this story for *The Guardian* in 2003, and like most stories it didn't end when the story was printed. The interesting part happened in the years after the mediation.

Tashi remained in the village and expanded her farming and ventured into other businesses. She leased some land and started a successful logging company. She bought a truck and has branched out into distribution, working with one of her sons.

After a few years, Dorji met and married a young woman from a nearby village, and they live together in her family's house. They have a daughter who is now about five years old. The grudges didn't last, and Tashi, Dorji, and Dorji's wife are friendly. Not only that, but from the moment of her birth, Dorji's little daughter and Tashi developed a special bond, so much so that Tashi is in fact raising the child.

Family situations like this aren't all that unusual in Bhutan and it speaks to the idea that in reality nothing ends in this world, especially marriages that produce children. The Bhutanese are practical and they have equanimity in spades. They might lose their tempers—after all, they're human. But something in their upbringing or their society or their DNA brings them around. It makes them calm and levelheaded and able to see clearly and they instinctively gravitate to the middle path. This isn't always the case, but it seems true in so many family situations. I know several happily married Bhutanese who started off married to other people, specifically brothers or sisters of their spouses. When it was clear that the brother or sister wasn't a good match, the husband or wife married other members of the same family. And everyone gets along. This would be unusual in the U.S., of course.

Don't go too far one way or the other; don't do too much or too little. Eat, drink, sleep, work, play, do everything and anything, but do it in moderation. Talk when necessary, not too much or too little. Practice self-control, temperance, and fairness. Watch your tendency to be loutish when you encounter someone who has opinions different than yours, curb your passion for always being right, and quit trying to control everything. Maintain equanimity with everything you do or say, even in pursuit of the middle path. It is a life's work.

About 20 years ago, the fourth king of Bhutan said that for his people he would rather have Gross National Happiness than Gross National Product. And so this seemingly whimsical declaration during an interview gave rise to a plan for developing the country. No decision can be made by the government of Bhutan unless it includes two of four "markers" or "indicators." Whatever is proposed by the government must be economically sound; it must help to preserve the environment; it must help promote the cultural tradition of the people; or it must be in keeping with good governance. Often the government will forgo economic gains if they lower the quality of life in other ways. That's why there's not a lot of heavy industry in Bhutan, a country rich in natural resources; the only thing that industry would improve is the economy. It wouldn't help the environment, the culture, or the government.

So in this way the newly democratized government of Bhutan follows the middle path. Although it is one of the least developed in the world, it's the only country (besides Cuba) with free health care and education. Bhutan is an example of a country that isn't rich but does a lot of things right. Its development program is a model for the rest of the world. I've read economists who weigh in on the subject and say that the idea is unrealistic. How realistic is it to base entire economies solely on economic indicators? How well is that working?

To move to the middle you have to decide what's important *besides* money.

I suppose my whole life I've lived a version of Gross National Happiness in that I don't necessarily do things just for money, and what I do has to hit several indicators. It needs to make me laugh, it needs to be compassionate, educational, or otherwise enriching, and if it's financially rewarding that's also good. The times in my life I've been least successful or fulfilled are the times when I'm just doing something for money.

Coming back to Nashville from Bhutan is like jumping off a bicycle that's still in motion, or getting off one of those moving airport walkways—we have to speed up to stay on our feet. Friends talking about their lives, the cars they drive, their plans and politics—it all seems deeply fascinating, but I have a hard time getting on board. It's like coming into a lecture on particle physics that's already half over. You've read the homework chapter but it's still a little fuzzy. But you know what? Part of me likes the feeling. I'm here but I'm not. Actually, I'm kind of in the middle. There are so many more ways to communicate in the U.S.; everyone has a cell phone and we're all hyper connected. There are hundreds of ways to express ideas, and access to food, clothing, shelter, and information is super easy. As long as I can occasionally cut through the clutter and simulate that slow, sweet existence I have in Bhutan when I'm in Nashville or elsewhere, then all is well. It's the best of both worlds.

On the other hand the events of September 11 onward have made fear palpable in the U.S. People's attitudes have changed. We are more cynical, and we're polarized. You're with us or against us. If you watch the news or surf the Internet you'll get plenty of bad news and it's as if the whole of the U.S. is having a slow nervous breakdown.

When I come to the U.S. after hanging out in Bhutan, I have a strong sense that we could all be fine if we'd just recapture more in our lives and in our experiences that gives us a sense of peace and a sense of acceptance. It really is a matter of taking on and disposing of habits, and doing some small, simple things well. Being a part of a community helps. We need more fun and we need to dial down the fear. Fear will always be with us. We just have to remember to move to the middle.

THERE ARE
NO ACCIDENTS

I'd lived in Bhutan for almost three years and Namgay and I were friends at the Painting School, where we both taught. He began coming to tea at my house in the afternoons and slowly, gradually, we relaxed into friendly banter. We had three months of winter holiday from school, so when he wasn't painting he would visit me at home. I learned to talk less and let big chunks of time go by without saying anything. It was the Bhutanese way. Buddha said that one shouldn't make idle chatter and should only speak when there is something to say. I'm not very good at this.

It was a cold winter but we were making our own heat source sitting in front of the wood stove and then later sitting huddled on two stools, knee to knee, in front of the tower heater in the sitting room, edging ever closer to the bedroom.

We hardly ventured outside of my house. It seemed the thing to do to just focus on each other and learn each other's language. He was, and is, a good cook. So often he would bring some nice vegetables or fresh mushrooms, something to make into curry to put over rice. I cooked pasta and taught him to steam vegetables. It was a great way to get to know each other and to expand our respective vocabularies in Dzongkha and English.

I kept a pile of English-Dzongkha dictionaries on a table beside the wood stove and if we were stuck cooking or conversing we'd go to the dictionaries and point at words.

We were not only formulating our own personal history but also describing, as each of us saw it, the history of the world, and in that sense we were creating a sort of cosmology, as married people—or people who are getting married—do. Namgay had never learned world history. Of course, he knew there was a very large world outside of Bhutan, but he hadn't watched television and his very focused education had included the Tantric Buddhist world, but not much else. So, we told each other what we knew.

He told me the first hereditary monarch of Bhutan, Ugyen Wangchuck, came to power at the turn of the 20th century, on December 17, 1907, in Punakha Dzong. His coronation ended the complex feuding in the region and brought a golden age to Bhutan.

I told him the rest of the world was in a big mess at that time. Anarchists, like present-day terrorists, were planting bombs all over Europe, and seven years later the First World War broke out. While soldiers in Normandy were swimming to the beaches and digging trenches, Ugyen Wangchuck's Bhutan was, for the first time in hundreds of years, peaceful.

When the North and South were fighting the Civil War against each other in the United States, Jigme Namgyel, the Black Regent and father of the first king, was fighting the British in the Duar War. And after five months of fighting, the Bhutanese lost the disputed territory to the British.

I told Namgay about the Crusades, which were during the time of Drukpa Kuenley and Pema Lingpa. When Shabdrung Ngawang Namgyal was unifying Bhutan, Michelangelo was painting the Sistine Chapel.

It was a lot to absorb, each other's histories along with the history of the world as we knew it. When Namgay was young he'd go to the movie theater in Thimphu and watch Charlie Chaplin movies—*The Great Dictator, Modern Times*. He knew them well, and he asked me where Chaplin lived.

"In Hollywood," I said. "That's in California. Or maybe London, in England. I'm not sure." He said he'd like to meet him, so I didn't mention that he was dead, and had been for some time. What would be the point of that?

Living high up in these insulated valleys I like the idea that we can have a bird's-eye view of the world, a broad perspective that lets us see and understand the connections of things. My life with Namgay confirms for me that there are no accidents and that we are all connected. The first time I came to Bhutan in 1994, a man gave me a ride on his motorcycle in Punakha. It was my first visit to Bhutan and I kept coming back. Three years later I moved to Bhutan and three years after that Namgay and I married. So it was a shock to me, after having been married for two years, to find out that I had met Namgay before, on my *first* trip to Bhutan. He was the man who gave me a ride on his motorcycle. I think about it all the time, and now I look for connections in things, and for *lagniappes*—a word I love, which means "unexpected gifts."

When we talked about marriage, Namgay was convinced that it was meant to be, because even though we came from such different parts of the world we met each other. Sometimes I think about all of the things that happen in our lives and wonder if we're not missing other connections, other events that are important. Deepak Chopra said, "There are no accidents . . . only patterns we haven't yet recognized." I'm certain this is true.

My marriage to Namgay has been a combination of extremes. Being with him is in some ways infinitely grounding. He is so self-possessed, and even. But the world encroaches. And there is nothing that makes me look for the hidden connections in things like when Namgay and I leave Bhutan and come to the U.S. I'm always looking for points of reference.

Back in Bhutan, Namgay and I sometimes go to a meditation center where his cousin Rinchen, a lama, lives. We like to visit him and spend the day there, so we park the car on the side of the road about four kilometers from a nearby pass. It's about a two-hour hike into the mountains to the center, which consists of a temple, a *shedra* (or monk school), and 15 or so small huts, isolated from one another, where devotees live in semi-seclusion and meditate. It's an important center for sacred activity.

The well-worn path follows the wide arc of a ridge, thick with forest cover. Mountain streams cut through the path and down into the steep valley below. We walk surrounded by trees; we can't see the valley floor. Lichen drips from the vegetation in the forest, and when we went this particular time, so many wildflowers, wild orchids, and strange plants I don't know the names of bordered the trail.

We always bring provisions for Rinchen, and a few treats, as he only infrequently makes it down the mountain. Of course, his family makes sure he has enough to eat and is well taken care of. Once, in winter, the trail was covered in ice and Namgay carried everything in his backpack because I was afraid I'd slip. As we slid our way up the side of the mountain, Namgay said I looked like RoboCop because I was walking without bending my legs to try to keep from falling on the icy path, holding my arms out for balance. I started talking like RoboCop to amuse him. We laughed all the way up the mountain.

This time, before we set off walking, we stopped to give a lift to an old *anim*, a nun. When she got in the car she and Namgay chatted. He asked her if the bears were active. They usually forage in late summer so they can get ready to hibernate, and it's a good idea to be alert and make noise on the trail. Namgay is always worried about bears and doesn't like to go into the woods when they're getting ready to hibernate. He's not paranoid; he's seen his share of friends and family who were mauled by bears. The old anim said that there were no bears. In fact, the bears seemed to have disappeared.

That was a relief. Himalayan black bears are aggressive. The Bhutanese believe if a farmer chases a bear from his fields, the bear will remember for up to nine years and seek retribution. With no bears to worry about, I quit paying attention, but then I thought I heard the word *monkeys*. Namgay exclaimed *"Pa, pa, pa, pa!"* Which roughly translated means something like "Holy shit!" After a while, the old anim indicated she wanted to be let out. After we dropped her off, I asked him what she said.

"Monkeys attacked a monk on the trail last week," he reported grimly.

"Is the monk okay?" I asked.

"No. Not okay," he said.

From Namgay's description, the monkeys had attacked without provocation. They'd bitten the monk's hand, face, and neck—they'd missed his carotid artery by centimeters, almost as if they were aiming for it. One monkey bit a two-inch chunk out of the monk's hand, in the flesh and muscle between thumb and forefinger. He almost bled to death before he made it to the road and a truck driver got him to the hospital. Monkey bites are efficient and nasty. Monkeys are killing machines.

Why have I gotten myself into this situation? I thought, walking up to Rinchen's. It's how things happen. You have a plan to do something, and then some new information comes to light and without thinking you carry on. Then you get in trouble.

Living in the mountains of Bhutan reinforces for me there are no accidents in life. If it's your time to get some bad juju then you just will. If it's your time to die, then you'll die; if not, you won't. Fatalism can be useful. But I also believe you can mitigate the bad stuff that happens to you by being careful, by not being too reckless. What's the difference between taking a healthy chance and making a reckless decision? Damned if I know. It's tied to synchronicity, the idea that two things that happen have subtle connections—maybe not causal connections, but connections nonetheless. You run into your college roommate in Italy, and it's just after you've thought about her or had a dream about her.

If we hadn't encountered the nun we wouldn't have known about the monkeys, and we wouldn't have been hypervigilant. So does this mean we had an edge on not encountering the monkeys or being attacked by them because we knew about them? Like I say, I think a lot about these things because I have this unlikely marriage.

We shouldn't avoid doing something just because it might have a little risk to it. What I really believe is that some kind of fate, or force of the universe, or karma has a hand in determining what comes around and goes around. If you put out goodwill, goodwill seeks you out—most of the time. Yet I know from living in nature that nature is random. Humans have no authority over it. We just have to adapt ourselves to it. And get used to not having that much control. There are powers higher than human powers. We are small in the universe.

When we reached his house on the side of a mountain, Rinchen wasn't there. He couldn't have gone far, so we took off our backpacks and waited. Namgay hiked over to a building site where workers were building a lama's new house. They told us Rinchen went to wash his clothes.

We opened some biscuits and had a few, and fed his two happy dogs, and in about 15 minutes he came with a basket of wet laundry. As he hung his maroon monk's robes and yellow shirts to dry on the line outside his house, he chatted with Namgay, and I wandered in his small, neat garden. He had hot pink dianthus and red poppies everywhere. There was one giant wall of sweet peas near the gate. They gave off a thickly sweet smell. Interspersed with the flowers were vegetables—mustard greens, peas, cilantro, chilies, tomatoes, and green beans.

Inside we sat on cushions on the floor of a small room that overlooked the valley a few kilometers away. Many temples dotted the hillside among the houses and small farms. If it were anyplace other than Bhutan nobody would live there, as the hillside is quite steep. But there are very few flat places in Bhutan. And the mountains invite meditation and reflection.

Rinchen has a handsome, round face and wears a red cap on his shaved head in summer or winter. His large, black eyes have a direct, almost piercing gaze, and they always seem to be smiling. I have rarely seen him when he didn't have a smile on his face; he always looks a little amused—as if he's in on some big cosmic joke that he wouldn't mind telling you if you asked. I think he is blissed-out. He's done two retreats, which means twice he's gone up into a cave and meditated for three years, three months, three weeks, and three days (and I suppose three hours, three minutes, and three seconds, although I don't know for sure), without any contact with other humans. That's a total of six and a half years in isolation and meditation. That must do a lot to change someone's worldview. Now he lives in the retreat, which is a simple house on the side of a mountain, and he meditates day and night. Sometimes he comes to Thimphu, to see family or help with a puja.

I find being in his presence relaxing and revitalizing. To say he is grounded would be an understatement. Inside his small house the mood was happy and light.

I have never met anyone who seems to be on the one hand so earthly and grounded, and on the other so eso-teric and otherworldly. This is, I believe, the essence of Buddhism—to contain opposites. Sometimes I think he's gone to another place and we're sitting with his earthly remains; he's in the world but not of the world.

My first reaction when we sat down in his little ante-room with windows on two sides was great relief, followed quickly by the urge to cry. I chalked it up to hormones, the physical exertion of the hike, worrying about the monkeys. I dabbed my eyes and breathed in the crisp mountain air and the feeling subsided. I felt calm.

I felt Rinchen must have known something about me, maybe even better than I knew myself—known without knowing. His gentle presence made me take deep breaths. Here, away from the world, I felt relaxed but exposed. I feel this way a lot with people in Bhutan who have chosen to live a devout, spiritual life on the fringes of society. I suppose they would be considered hermits. They don't struggle with the things of this world like we do. I can sense their compassion. Because they stand outside of society, they are good observers, and they understand the toll it exacts to live in the world among people.

As Rinchen moved around the place serving us tea, his floor-length red robes flowed, and it seemed a wonderful, flamboyant touch, a nice contrast to this simple life. While I sat in a semi-meditation, he and Namgay chatted. Namgay unloaded our packs: oil for the butter lamps, incense, prayer flags, tea, biscuits, mangoes, and *zow*—baked crunchy rice. The last time we were in the U.S., at Costco, Namgay bought a canvas lunch pack with insulated bags so that food could be kept hot or cold for several hours. These are ubiquitous in the U.S., but we couldn't get them in Bhutan. I had heated the plastic, gel-filled bags in boiling water so the *momos*, Tibetan steamed dumplings filled with cheese and cabbage, were hot when we served them to Rinchen.

I unzipped the blue bag and steam came out. "What black magic is this?" Rinchen said, laughing with genuine surprise. His reality encompassed such simple things—simple physical things, that is. He had no indoor water and had only recently gotten electricity—a couple of dim bulbs. Wires from a box outside the house went to the ceiling of his prayer room, and one lit the kitchen. It was so much fun to amaze him with a thing that we had grown to accept as mundane. Namgay, schooled by late-night infomercials in the U.S., explained how the gelatinous bags in the side pockets of the carrier kept things hot or cold, as Rinchen looked on with artless delight.

Throughout the summer he'd lived on rice and whatever grew in his garden. He went at the momo with real appreciation, plopping a whole one into his mouth. Namgay and I claimed we weren't hungry and only ate a few of the momos. That way there would be enough for Rinchen to eat more after we'd gone.

When they get together, Rinchen and Namgay always tell the story of when they were young. They were best friends, cousins, and went everywhere together. They always had the idea to go into the monkhood. They would go together, they said, and when the time came, they bought monks' robes in Thimphu and went to tell their uncle, a lama. He congratulated Rinchen, but he told Namgay that he shouldn't become a monk. Instead he should go to study at the Painting School and become a thangka painter. I've heard them both tell the story at different times and each time they do it, they smile in the same wistful way and laugh. See? No accidents.

We spent the afternoon in the sunny room, talking some, but mostly relaxing and putting our faces to the bright window with our eyes closed.

Then it was time to go.

As we were leaving, Rinchen reminded us about the monkeys.

"If they have babies with them, they will attack," he said in a matter-of-fact way.

A nice send-off, I thought. And if it had been anyone else I would have said something sarcastic: "Easy for you to say," or "Thanks, you have a great day, too." See, this is the thing: this wouldn't be happening in the world I grew up in. We would have gotten animal control to shoot darts into the monkeys, or we would have killed them all off long ago or put them in zoos. It really is a different way of being in the world.

Rinchen walked us to the trailhead and we said our good-byes. He had an Indian sweet, a treasure wrapped in bright blue paper, and smiled as he pressed it into my hand. We walked away and I turned around just as the path veered to the left. He was far away by then, but I could see him standing there as still as a tree.

It was about 4:30, later than we'd planned to leave, and the sun was going behind the mountains, making long, dramatic shadows. It gets chilly fast without much sun. My body felt tight from walking and listening for the monkeys.

"We should hurry," said Namgay. "It's getting dark." We had another hour of walking to get to the car.

"When the going gets tough, the tough get going," I said to Namgay.

"What did you say?"

I repeated it.

"That's a good one," he said.

One great thing about being married to Namgay is that I can use worn-out clichés and he thinks they sound fresh and original.

We walked along, not wanting to talk but needing to make noise to scare off the monkeys. "Rinchen's reaction to the hot case was AMAZING!" I said, but it fell flat.

Namgay said he'd left the case with Rinchen.

"Are you sad you didn't become a monk with Rinchen?" I asked.

"Sometimes," he said. And he did a little Charlie Chaplin walk that was both charming and heartbreaking. After a moment he said, "Charlie Chaplin lived a long time ago." He looked back at me and smiled.

We've always had a thing between us; even before we married, when we were sitting by the wood stove that cold winter talking about our lives, planning, getting to know each other, Namgay said when he got older he wanted to go into meditation—do that three-year retreat thing.

"What about me?" I'd always say. There was no immediate answer from him, only, "It won't be for a long time."

Now it's been a long time. I used to joke that when we got older we'd buy a time-share at a monastery. "I don't think I could live like Rinchen," I said.

"I know," Namgay said.

Screeching in the forest above interrupted us. The monkeys were there. It sounded like hundreds of them, although I knew it was fewer than that. But it wouldn't take many. I was scared.

"Namgay!" I cried.

"Come! Hurry!" he said, holding out his hand to me.

I was a few yards behind him on the trail and I ran toward him—more like leapt to him—and grabbed his hand.

"Namgay!" I cried again. "They're here!" We ran together along the trail. My legs have never gone so fast, but even so I felt him pulling me.

Then, from the depths of hell or an abyss or some tortured place there came the most unearthly, forlorn animal howl. It started low like a growl and then it rose up like a yell. It took me a second to realize it was coming from Namgay. He didn't sound human or like anything I had ever heard before or since. The only thing I could think was it sounded like grief. Pure, unfathomable grief.

What it sounded like to the monkeys I have no idea. But they quit their screeching and evaporated into the forest cover.

LEARN TO
BE WATER

In the U.S. and in Bhutan we always seem to live in places with water nearby. Namgay and I have a large, slow pond in our front yard in the States chock-full of dopey, fat bass hiding in its shoals. In Thimphu, I can hear the glacier-runoff river roaring down the hill behind our house. It's funny how the water in each place is directly opposite to the societies' sensibilities there.

Fed by rains in summer, our river in Bhutan rushes over rocks and makes rapids, and the noise of the water blends in a lovely way with the syllabic sounds of Namgay's evening prayers: *om ah hung*. The constant water sound is soothing, and it also is a reminder to flow. *Go, flow*, it says. Disturbances can't stop you or trip you up. You just go around them or under them or over them. Or stop and take a shape until that shape changes. Everything is temporary. The flow is the thing. Lie back into it and see where it takes you.

"Go with the flow" has been my mantra ever since I came to Bhutan. My ways are not the Bhutanese ways, which is why it's all the more important for me to suppress my natural, American, get-all-up-in-your-face pushing and elbowing my way through life. Living in Bhutan is more like treading water, or just lying back on a big rubber raft. Back in the States I have to remind myself to step it up, commandeer, take charge, punch it, kick ass, get up and go 0 to 60. The Bhutanese way of doing things translated into Americanese seems too passive, even overly submissive. Going from here to there is like turning a water spigot. It takes energy to turn a trickle into a torrent and then back again. Either place, whatever the flow, it seems important to go with it. I gush and surge in the U.S.; in Bhutan I kick back and float, glide, or coast with the gentle under-lying current that carries us all. It's not to say there aren't obstructions in Bhutan. Oh no, far from it. But we have to learn to be water. I hear these words in my head all the time. "Learn to Be Water" is the title as well as the first line of a poem by Morton Marcus. I read it when I was in high school and, unlike the rest of the poem, which I've lost track of, those words always stuck with me.

Here, gentle readers, is a fable:

Once upon a time there was a woman who loved many things in this world. She loved her family, she loved a certain pair of jeans that made her look tall and sleek with her Cordani boots, she loved the way the clouds poured over the mountains during summer monsoons, she loved hiking in the mountains with her daughter, and she loved eating chocolate cake at the Art Café with her friend Louise while talking about losing weight. Most of all she loved her washing machine. Yes, it's true, her washing machine was right up there in the top four or five things she loved most. That's because she liked to be clean, and deep down inside she was terrified of washing by hand. Terrified, because it would take an excruciatingly long time—at least one whole day out of each week of her life—to do laundry for a family of three. That would be beyond boring, and it would take real, bona fide muscle and excellent upper body strength to wring out a machine load of terry cloth bath towels and hang them on the line. It made her tired just thinking about it. Having clean clothes was very high up on her list of things that separated her from the lower primates. In fact, she felt as if her washing machine was a sort of glue that held her somewhat chaotic life together. She lived in a remote Himalayan country most of the year, where most of the people washed their clothes in streams or in buckets, and so she felt very fortunate. In fact, of the seven billion people inhabiting the planet, only two billion have access to washing machines. That's less than a third of the people in the world who can wash their clothes in a machine. The rest wash by hand, if they have water. If they don't have water, not even a machine can help them get clean, which is terrible to think about. But you know it happens.

One day she went to take some darks, mostly jeans and T-shirts, out of the machine, and she could see from the round glass window at the front of the machine that it was full of stagnant water. All its lights were on, but nothing was moving. The clothes floated, limp and helpless, drowning in a soapy brew. She panicked and ran to her husband.

"Something's wrong! The washing machine is broken!" Anguish and dread welled up in her. Her heart raced.

Her husband looked at the machine, punched some buttons, unplugged it, plugged it back in, checked the fuse box, walked around the machine again, scratched his head, and said, "I don't know what's wrong."

These dreadful, hideously terrifying words shook her to the very core of her being. "Can you get someone to fix it?" she asked.

"I don't know," he said, scratching his crotch. "What to do, la?" he added.

When Bhutanese people don't know what to do they say, *What to do, la?* The horse won't go up the hill. *What to do, la?* The car won't start. *What to do, la?* The washing machine is broken, and so on . . . It is not an exclamation of defeat. Rather, it is an acknowledgment that there are forces at work—karmic forces, if you will—that make something impossible, or at least difficult. Forces that can stop you in your tracks or just delay you. It is an acceptance of fate and the inevitability of things to go all Murphy's Law on us. *What to do, la?* Nothing, really. Just live with it. Flow with it. Move on to something else.

This was not music to her ears. She had laughingly referred to the washing machine as the love of her life, many times, to many people, because it made her life so easy. She'd even written those very words in a book. It had served her for over ten years, and I don't want to sound too much like I'm doing a commercial here, but it really got her clothes clean. Absolutely no complaints. It was shipped from the U.K. as part of a household allowance of her sainted Scottish friends, Roger and Sarah, who worked at an NGO in Thimphu. They gave it to her as they departed Bhutan many years before. She gave them some rugs and Bhutanese furniture and a painting by her husband. But now, on that infamous day, it just refused to work. It had never done this before and she chastised herself for not paying attention, for not tending to it as it deserved. Maybe it had been sick and she just didn't pay attention.

She was devastated, especially because she and her husband had taken a trip to Tsirang over the previous weekend and had a lot of dirty clothes. In fact, they hadn't used the machine in about a week, and many of their clothes, towels, and sheets had piled up. One thing she and her husband could always agree on was the need to be clean. They were both pretty shaken.

Her husband called the electrician, who didn't know when he'd be able to come—maybe Tuesday. This was Saturday. Three anxious days hand-washing underwear and T-shirts passed. The electrician arrived the morning of the fourth day and the husband set about making a big lunch for him, as was his custom when anybody, even a random stranger, or friends, or friends of friends, or, I don't know, possibly even a stray dog came to the house. I mean he will just drop anything he's doing and make an elaborate meal using the best of whatever is in the kitchen, even some nice dried beef that she had been saving for a special occasion. Or if there's nothing suitable in the house he'll go down to the market and pick up a nice plump chicken, bring it home, and cook it. But she didn't mind because she easily and effortlessly had learned to go with most anything that was happening. She flowed. She visualized the electrician finishing his ample lunch and then fixing the machine in about five minutes. See? She was flowing.

The electrician, in a grimy gho and shoes with no socks, belched extravagantly as he tipped the machine on its side, and after poking around its underbelly and taking off the back panel and poking around there, pronounced that a belt had broken. Did washing machines still have belts? Never mind. *A belt isn't that big of a deal,* she thought. The machine would be fixed by nightfall, most probably. This was just a minor inconvenience. If life were a stream, then this was no more than a little rock that was plunked down in the middle of it. She could just go around it.

Her husband went to Doma Enterprise, the only actual appliance store in town, to find a replacement belt. The manager was happy to see him because the husband had bought a big refrigerator from the store a few weeks before, but he said that the store no longer carried belts. He directed the husband to a nice, new Indian washing machine available for purchase. Perhaps he thought the husband was made of money. The husband wasn't going to give up that easily, though, and when the manager stepped to the back of the store to answer the phone, a young Indian salesman told him that there was a place near the vegetable market, above the meat stall, that might have a belt for the washing machine. A man who lived there imported belts from Bangladesh, and there might be one that would fit.

The husband hastened to the vegetable market and after much wandering around, and many discussions with proprietors of shops, he found out the belt man had gone to see his father in Trashigang in Eastern Bhutan . . . carrying with him the key to the cupboard where the belts were stored. The man's father was ill and old, but alive. Alive was the good news. The bad news was there was no way to tell how long the belt salesman would be gone. In other words, it might take the old man awhile to die.

Coming out of the shop, the husband met a relative (we'll call him Sonam Gyetlshen), who was trying to track down a mutual friend. The husband hadn't seen the friend in a while, he told the relative. Never mind. Sonam invited the husband to his house for late lunch. At lunch, Sonam's wife served lettuce from her garden, and she had what the husband later described to his wife as the greatest, most amazing, most extraordinarily useful thing ever created in the history of the world: a salad spinner. The husband had never seen one and was somehow stunned that you could wash lettuce, put it in the spinner, and, using centrifugal force, dry the salad. You could even store the lettuce in the spinner. You have to understand that when the husband is in the U.S., one of his favorite things to do is to stay up all night painting and watching infomercials. The combination of American ingenuity, cheesy presenters, and cheap Chinese appliances endlessly amazes him. The truth is he and his wife take turns washing lettuce in their home by putting it in a pillow case designated for the purpose, and going outside on the porch and vigorously rotating the pillowcase filled with lettuce over their heads to dry it. A salad spinner was way more elegant and efficient and wouldn't tend to baptize the person spinning the lettuce. He asked where to find a salad spinner and Sonam directed him to a shop near the bus stop across from Chang Lam Plaza. The husband finished his lunch, thanked his hosts, and hustled over to Chang Lam Plaza.

Meanwhile, the wife remained at home and sat at her desk staring at the screen saver on her computer. She resolved to remain optimistic. The husband would find the belt that would allow the beloved washing machine to operate. He was infinitely resourceful, after all. He knew things. He was Bhutanese. She was from another country far away, and her people were generally an impatient and pessimistic lot, accustomed to having things operate smoothly and getting hung up when they didn't. But not her. She flowed.

Late in the afternoon the husband returned. He came into the house in a burst of energy, a bulging plastic bag in his hand.

"Look at this!" he said, pulling the thing out of the bag.

The wife was confused. "You're fixing the washing machine with a salad spinner?" she asked.

He'd completely forgotten about the washing machine belt. Believe me when I tell you that at that moment in time the wife wanted to push her husband into the raging river behind the house. She had waited over a week to get her beloved washing machine fixed. She had spot cleaned, washed by hand, and even washed out a couple of towels that very afternoon, and the clothes she was wearing were frankly less than clean. She felt like her husband had turned into Jack from *Jack and the Beanstalk*, the boy whose mother sent him to town to sell a cow and he came back with magic beans.

"You love salad," he said, sounding a little dejected.

It was then she realized that getting angry would do no good. She let things flow because she was learning to be water. Instead of chastising her husband, she decided to pretend she found his enthusiasm for the salad spinner charming. She decided to enjoy the moment, pick some lettuce from the garden, wash it, and, what the hell, spin it. At least something in the house would be clean. This was Bhutan, where things like salad spinners and garlic presses and other conveniences were hard to find.

They enjoyed a nice big salad for dinner.

And here's the greatest thing: The next day the husband found an inner tube at his sister's house, because she's a little bit of a hoarder, thank God, and using the broken washing machine belt as a prototype, he and his brother-in-law "fabricated" a belt for the washing machine with epoxy and a staple gun. It fit into the washing machine perfectly, and the washing machine was revived and lived to clean another day. Now, five years later, it's still cleaning. Water flows in and out of it, as do clothes, towels, and sheets. It remains an excellent machine. And the husband and wife still have the salad spinner, too.

The wife is so happy every time she keeps her cool. She's proud, really, because she's learned it all usually works out, one way or the other. She expects hardship because she lives in Bhutan and has an intercultural marriage, a 16-year-old daughter, and a dodgy career as a writer. Sometimes she goes to the U.S. and has a different set of challenges like forgetting which side of the road to drive on, but that's only happened two or three times.

Bhutan changed my life, but not in the ways I expected. Moving to or from a place won't change who you are, I understand, and it won't necessarily make you happier. But the huge value added of moving and traveling, or staying put and just training yourself to think differently, is that you can learn and you can take on new habits and ideas. I got a whole world full of new ideas in Bhutan that I can use anywhere, and I learned to take life as it comes, however it comes. To get to a simpler level of existence, to think differently about time, to live with more grace and humor, to adapt yourself to your environment, to let go of control, to quit pushing so much—this is learning to flow, and this is what I learned living in Bhutan.

If you can do this, taking risks—doing big, crazy, fantastic things—will seem completely doable. If you get stuck, then go in another direction. But keep going. Keep moving. Then you won't get stuck. There will always be flux and obstacles. Like water in the river, I know that flow is the thing. A place can't really change your essence. Nothing can. But a place can most definitely shape you. And you can shape yourself to fit the place. You have to keep going, even when things get rocky. *What to do, la?* Never stop.

Let it go. Let it be. Let it flow.

DON'T EXPECT
EVERYTHING TO
ALWAYS WORK OUT

For years I lived in Bhutan as a perpetual guest. I had to renew my visa every few months. There was always a new rule or process, another hoop to jump through, another glitch, a new twist, and a moment in the process when I felt as though things wouldn't work out. But at the last minute it would. It used to make me so anxious, but somehow I reached a level of tranquility, a sense that everything will work out, one way or the other. And if it doesn't? Well, sometimes it's when things don't go according to plan that life gets interesting.

It's a hard lesson for Westerners. We have staked our claim to the concept of "expecting." *I expect it will be a long trip; I look forward to visiting with you; Let's look ahead to the market's projections; I await your response. I don't anticipate any problems. Wait for it* . . . See? We do a lot of projecting. We schedule everything. I haven't found any statistics to back this up, but I'd be willing to bet over half our thoughts are projections and expectations about the future. The Bhutanese cultural proclivities are to not get all hung up about what's going to happen in a few minutes, a few days, or a few years. They have lots of intent and determination, but they're not quite so invested in the outcome.

The way the Bhutanese drive on the narrow, winding road that curves across the country is a perfect example of their ability to adapt quickly and not sweat the small stuff. Talk about living in the moment! As they guide the vehicle, guests in the backseat claw the upholstery and clench their butt cheeks, astounded at the difficulty of getting from point A to point B, and wishing they'd brought clean underwear.

At first I could not fathom the very real danger and the sheer acrobatics the driver and we passengers had to go through every time we had to go somewhere. The road was a lane and maybe just a little wider in places—say a lane and a half—so it was inevitable to come face-to-face with huge trucks, or families of five balancing together like acrobats on a tiny scooter, or a vegetable vendor who had imprudently set her wares in the middle of a blind curve. A driver had to throw his or her whole body weight and a whole lot of intent into the brakes to avoid collision. Thank God for Bhutanese quick reflexes and their propensity to pray a lot. Everyone would let out a deep breath, back up, reposition, and slowly inch forward, folding their side mirrors so they wouldn't break off as truck and car crept past, inches from the chasm on the side of the narrow mountain road.

A perpetual abyss on one side of you probably figures greatly in your ability to be a little mellow and circumspect. If it's your time to go off the side, there's not much you can do about it. Bhutanese drivers have very low pressure points because they don't anticipate everything going smoothly, or going any way, really. They start and remain in the moment.

Hardships engender resilience, toughness, and buoyancy. You have to get your mind in the right place. I started thinking like this many years ago. I still have to work at it, but positive results come almost immediately if you don't anticipate so much on the front end. I drop a lot of attitude when I listen to some of the stories my Bhutanese friends tell me about their lives.

One Bhutanese woman I know has lived for almost nine decades and is still going strong. Married young, six children, she's had a full life. I used to visit her, and listen to her stories. I'd walk to the house where she lived with her daughter. I'd sit on a chair and she'd sit cross-legged on her bed in the temple room in her daughter's house that doubled as her bedroom. There were always cats sleeping on a pile of suitcases or a stack of blankets, and there were usually kittens around, too. She spoke slowly and thoughtfully, as if she was recollecting something from a long time ago. I learned she was a Buddhist nun in her youth, but then something happened that forever changed her path.

At her birth, as was the custom, her mother and father took her to a lama in the temple near their village, and he made an astrological chart based on the year, time, and place she was born. It predicted her life up until the time of her death, and it said she would live for many, many years, which has certainly come to pass. It said she would be a nun, and that's why the lama named her Lhamo, which means "holy person." Her parents were happy because it's auspicious to have clergy in the family, and a good way to stockpile some good karma for everybody.

When she was barely seven, still a small child, her parents took her to a nunnery deep in the hills above Punakha town to fulfill her destiny. It took three days from her village in Trongsa. There was no road, only a footpath. At night under the stars, she and her parents and an aunt and uncle sat around a big fire telling stories of lamas and holy men who subdued demons in the surrounding valley. It was a big thing to be going away from home. She had never been so far.

"Were you happy?" I asked, a Westerner's question.

She said yes; she wanted to be a nun. She thought about it all the time when she was young, and her uncle had even started to teach her classical *Choekay,* the Tibetan alphabet, so she could learn to interpret the holy texts and not just memorize them like most nuns in Bhutan. She knew what her life would be like; she was ready.

But she cried when her parents left her at the nunnery.

It was a very clean place with about 30 girls and some older women and an abbess. Mornings began with prayer, then study, then chores. They woke before dawn and went to bed when night fell. She loved to say her morning and evening prayers with the other novices at the nunnery. She was a quick student and learned all the lessons. *"Nga keta du,"* she said. (I was clever.)

It was a good place for Lhamo, and a good way to grow up—plenty of discipline; a regimented life; healthy food; a clean, spartan environment; a life of goodness and prayer. She said she loved to be in the temple best of all. She spent hours praying there, and when not in prayer, she cleaned it. She loved changing the flowers, pouring the seven sacred bowls of water every morning, making butter lamps, sweeping, all under the eyes of the massive gold Buddhas with their beatific smiles and enlightened, detached gazes. It must have been so pleasing to grow up looking at those faces.

"Every day we prayed for peace in the world," said Lhamo. "We prayed unceasingly."

When she was 20 she got very sick. She couldn't eat or sleep. She developed an agitated limp as a debilitating pain shot up her leg day and night. She sat under a tree on the nunnery grounds or she'd lie in bed, too weak to get up. She lost weight and couldn't concentrate. Her robes swallowed her. She was wasting away. Her world was ending as the life force drained out of her.

Out of desperation the abbess sent for her mother and father. By the time they arrived, Lhamo was too weak to sit up. Her mother started to cry. "It's all right. She'll get better," her father said. But of course he was worried. She was his only daughter. She could die.

It would have been around 1946, and there was no hospital or doctor or Western medicine. The only thing to do was to take her to a lama. So they did. Lhamo was terrified. She wasn't afraid of dying, but she was terrified because the beautiful faces she saw every day in the temple, the statues beaming down, no longer gave her comfort or peace. Pain was distracting her. Her stomach burned like a hot coal.

She'd become dizzy and nauseous and nothing, not prayers, nor the hot water and herbal remedies the other nuns brought her, nor the rice porridges, nor the lucky charms would do the slightest to ease the pain.

She could hardly think of prayer or meditation. Lhamo was afraid she was not a very good nun. She thought perhaps if she died, she could get a new, better body, and one that wouldn't give her so much pain. At least this was a comfort.

Lhamo's skin was becoming waxy and ashen and her bones had begun to protrude. She was already starting to look like a corpse. At that time in Bhutan it was no small feat to organize a two-day walk to see a lama, who might be able to help her. Her parents had to borrow a horse. There was great expense.

The lama was renowned for his healing abilities and lived in a monastery near their village. Arrangements had to be made, provisions had to be acquired, as well as things for the lama: fresh cow's milk, butter, eggs, dried plums, as well as food for the family that would make the trip.

He was much revered and it was said that he would sometimes go to live in a cave high above the temple, sometimes for years, to meditate. Some people also said he could change himself into a white bird; some said it was a raven.

The road to the lamasery became treacherous, because it was summer and there was mud and there were frequent landslides. At night they made Lhamo as comfortable as possible, making a bed for her with leaves and branches. When they got to the monastery the monks gave them tea and then fed them a meal of rice and chilies.

When Lhamo saw the lama she noted that he had the same face as the beautiful statues in the nunnery, only older and withered. But the eyes were the same. He smiled at her and gestured for her to come sit near him. Her mother and father helped her walk toward the lama. She sat down and he took her wrist using his thumb and forefinger. For what seemed like a long time, he held her wrist. His timeless eyes looked at her face, while she looked down and away, out of shyness and respect.

Then he took her hand in his for only an instant, and put it in her lap on top of her other hand. Lhamo's parents sat, looking, barely able to contain their anxiety. This lama was their only chance, their only hope. Lhamo's mother worked her beads and her lips moved with silent prayer.

Lhamo paused in her narration and looked down at a pile of kittens sleeping beside her on the bed. She looked at me and gave her shy smile. "Lama said I need . . ." Her voice trailed off. "I don't know how to say," she told me.

"*Ca?*" (What?) I asked in Dzongkha. I was confused.

"It's what the lama said . . . I don't . . ." she said, stopping in mid-sentence.

There is this language barrier. Sometimes when we're talking we have to call another family member who speaks English if there is an impasse.

I was thinking I had missed the thread of her narrative altogether and that I had gotten it all muddled.

"The lama gave you medicine?" I asked. She didn't reply. "Shall I call Namgay?" She seemed to be deep in thought.

"No! Don't call him! Call Karma!" she said.

I went to get her daughter, Karma. They chatted, heads together. Karma suddenly threw back her head and laughed.

Okay. This was interesting.

Karma looked at me. "She says tell you . . ." She paused. "Tell you 'man injection,'" Karma said, and she put the back of her hand on her mouth and laughed again.

"What did you say? Man what?" I'd misunderstood.

"She needed man injection," Karma said. She laughed again.

"Man? Injection? MAN injection?"

"Husband," Karma said brightly.

Both Lhamo and Karma sitting on the bed nodded in unison: yes. Now they both laughed; we all laughed. It was true. In olden times and probably now, there is a belief that some women can't live, will die even, without semen flowing in their bodies. That's a whole other book, and I have to say there's certainly a lot of Tantric stuff going on in Bhutan, and they have an unspoken attitude that if you're talking a lot about Tantric then you're probably not really doing it. It's a secret ritual, after all. So I knew that was all I'd probably get them to say about that.

So Lhamo got her diagnosis. She needed a man, and the lama took a wooden box from the table in front of him and pulled out what looked to be a small piece of dried meat. He handed it to Lhamo's mother. "She must take this. Make a tea with hot water," he said.

"Was it for your stomach?" I asked.

"No, it was for the man," she said.

It was magic to make the man come to her.

Back in the village, Lhamo started to get better. She'd left the nunnery for good. The burning in her stomach gradually subsided. Her hair grew back. In springtime, a man, a *gomchen,* or lay monk, in his long red robes and long wild hair did wander into the village and he did become Lhamo's husband.

"I have it here," she said, and touched the Tibetan pouch on the bench.

"Have what here?" I wondered. A snapshot of her husband coming along the trail?

No. It was the medicine that made her husband come to her, now a fine black powder, in a Ziploc bag.

She has no regrets, she says, no pangs or recriminations. Her life is an unbroken line. It didn't go the way she had expected, but being Bhutanese, she didn't live with that much anticipation of how it would be.

In work, relationships, spirituality, and the trappings of success, all of our social markers, we in the West do anticipate and hope for the best. We expect our cars to run and our lives to go smoothly. In fact, they do move pretty seamlessly, all things considered.

The Bhutanese seem to be able to embrace the concept of living, not only with less, but with less anticipation. Not expecting that everything will work out turns out to be a more optimistic way to live. It's stoic, yes, but in the end it makes me happier. Being as opposed to aspiring, living in the present, focusing on intent as opposed to outcome, is a good way to a more balanced life.

Chapter
17

THINK ABOUT DEATH FIVE TIMES A DAY

I have a confession. I think about death all the time. But I don't consider myself a maudlin person. Quite the contrary. Instead of making me gloomy and grim, preferring the company of ravens, listening to heavy metal, and wearing all black, thinking about death makes me feel lighter and funnier, and I embrace the ridiculous with ease. Thinking about death makes me want to live—not in the worst way, but in the best way.

Nothing makes me want to recommit my life and make every day count like losing a beautiful friend or public figure too soon, whether it's to cancer or a car accident, or something equally arbitrary. Death is ugly. But death is also beautiful in the sense that it gives us focus and reminds us to be mindful, present, exuberant, and to once and for all forget about things that don't matter. We don't have that much time. And it's going to happen to all of us.

My aunt is 90 and now she talks about going to be with her mother and father and her sisters. I like the way she thinks. It's like they're waiting for her at a table in Applebee's in heaven.

All over Bhutan we see images of death. There are statues, paintings, carvings, words, symbols, and photographs. You can see them in the temples, in homes, and in shops. They are even painted on the rocks. We see skulls with hollowed-out eyeballs, half skulls filled with brains, disemboweled people, flayed and burning bodies, and all manner of grisly images in the religious iconography. They are metaphors, reminders to be mindful. Death's unmistakable smell is all around, and in case your sinuses are blocked, if you look north just past Tashichhodzong, the enormous government center, monastery, and fortress in Thimphu, you can see the smoke billowing from the cremation grounds most every day.

Also it seems that there are so many ingenious, cinematic ways to die in Bhutan. There's dengue fever, which is mysterious and rather hard to diagnose and will take a person quietly with not much fuss in a day or two. I've known people who have been eaten by wild boars because they stepped off a trail to answer the call of nature; who have fallen off of, driven over, or been crushed by part of a falling mountain; or who have been compressed by a random, falling boulder while languishing in a hot spring. Exposure is always common, as are bear maulings. And every year, a family or two succumbs to poisoned mushrooms during August or September, which is high season for the fungus. But there's always an old grandfather or grandmother who doesn't like mushrooms or who has a little stomach thing and can't eat them, and so is left to tell the tale.

The road offers some rather ingenious ways to depart this life. Once, years ago, we were driving between Wangdue and Gangtey and saw a massive landslide, where a big chunk of earth separated and slid down the mountain and took a Maruti van with a family of four down into the valley with it. We had been following the van quite closely for several hours, and then—poof—it was gone.

I, too, have had brushes with death. In Mongar, photographing a 30-foot waterfall from the other side of a giant gorge, I got too close to the edge, but the quick reflexes of my driver, who was standing nearby, saved me. He grabbed my belt as my feet slipped off the cliff, and dragged me to safety. My camera went into the abyss. I was too shocked to cry, but not too shocked to pee in my pants. So much for dignity.

Driving from Wangdue to Gangtey has occasionally been unlucky for me. Once the brakes in our vehicle failed. Luckily, or unluckily, I wasn't driving. We let a tree and the hand brake stop us.

When I was 15 my father, a private pilot, had to force a landing after we took off from Washington, DC, because of a freak snowstorm. Sixty-mile-an-hour winds and ice on the wings depleted our fuel. As we descended, I asked, "Dad, are we going to die?" "Hahahahaha! Noooooo!" he said, way too jovially. That's when I knew we were doomed. I kept looking out at the wing, trying to convince myself that the ice on it was melting. Then he said, "Look for something soft and flat and inexpensive for us to land on." Luckily we found a spot. He was in constant radio contact, of course, and we were guided to a tiny airstrip in the mountains of North Carolina. We refueled, the snowstorm passed, and I sat, huddled on the steps of a trailer next to the dirt runway with great red welts all over my body. Hives. Again, so much for dignity. It took my father over three hours to convince me to get back in the plane.

But some things are actually worse than death. The one time in my life I can say I absolutely and positively no longer wanted to live was in eighth-grade Spanish class when I sneezed and accidentally farted really loud.

More seriously, I know that people who suffer a great deal from their own or other people's terminal illness, addiction, poverty, war, and ignorance lose the life force and believe that their lives are no longer worth living. And then some people have that force so strongly you can't imagine they could be anything but alive.

I believe that thinking about death, and by that I mean acknowledging that it exists and that it will happen to you one day, will actually make you happier. It will most certainly help you prepare for what's coming, and preparation is almost always a good thing. It will also assuage the fear we all have of the unknown. Anger, frustration, and confusion are also part of the mix of feelings we have if we really delve into it and think about our demise.

Our lives are so fragile, and we must make peace with the fact that we are going to die. I'm convinced that we in the West add so many useless things to our lives in an attempt to avoid this fact. We metaphorically barricade our houses with stuff in front of the door and barricade our lives to stave off death. Things are our distractions from thinking about what really matters, maybe because thinking about what really matters is troubling and scary. Because we're frightened, we load our lives with things we don't really need. We take on projects, ideas, thoughts, hopes, and worries, and load our days with busywork trying to distract ourselves from death. But it comes anyway. Ultimately, denial of death works against our happiness and well-being because in order to not deal with death, we give it a prominent place at the table. That is to say we spend so much time and energy avoiding it, trying not to be scared by it, that we are unable to enjoy life. We have to get familiar with it.

Something happened in 2003 that forever changed the way I look at death. There was a military action in Bhutan and the Bhutanese Army routed out thousands of Indian nationals who had been hiding in the dense jungles of southern Bhutan.

Historically and politically, the northeastern part of India, the area just below Bhutan, has never really been an enthusiastic part of the country. The history is long and involved, but suffice it to say its people are still desperately poor, tribal, and exploited. It's a Wild West kind of place, with porous borders and quite a bit of lawlessness, and for part of the 1980s and all of the 1990s, organizations like the ULFA, the Bodos, Maoist rebels, and hundreds of other anti-Indian paramilitary organizations wanting to secede from India hid from the Indian authorities in the dense, almost impassable, and underpopulated southern jungles of Bhutan. They set up camps for combat training and conducted raids into India, bombing train stations, attacking vehicles, and generally making life difficult for the Assamese and Bengalis. They also made life very difficult for about 65,000 Bhutanese living in the south. For six years the Bhutanese government tried negotiating with the rebels who were hiding. The Royal Government even tried paying them to leave. The rebels took the money but still refused to budge.

Finally, the Indian government said if the Bhutanese didn't kick out the rebels, then the Indian Army would come and do it themselves. We all knew that once the Indian Army came into Bhutan it would never leave. It's essentially what happened to Sikkim, Bhutan's neighbor, when Nepali insurgents overran the country.

Then, something mythic happened, something so large and remarkable and bigger than life that it really only happens in the movies or in Shakespeare's plays. We were accustomed to the hands-on leadership of King Jigme Singye Wangchuck, the then 48-year-old fourth hereditary monarch. But in mid-December 2003, we were collectively stunned when he left Thimphu for the southern districts to lead 6,000 Bhutanese soldiers into battle against the Indian rebels. Stop a moment and think of a world leader you know—the leader of a country or an organization like the UN, the CEO of a company, the head of a university—who would actually, personally, lead an army into battle. I can't think of anyone but the Bhutanese king.

The fighting officially began on December 14. The Bhutanese Army attacked all 30 of the rebel camps in a simultaneous raid early that morning, and two days later the bulk of the conflict was over thanks to the surprise attack. The rebels were rounded up and put on buses and in trucks and driven into India and remanded to the Indian Army. Across the river from our farm is the Army base outside of Thimphu, where Indian helicopters brought the bodies of dead Bhutanese soldiers, 11 in all.

Even more extensive than the military campaign, and every bit as focused, was the enormous civilian campaign of prayers and pujas conducted throughout the country, to appease the protector deities and compel them to save the troops and His Majesty, and even the Indian rebels, and keep the sovereignty of Bhutan. All of the doctors and many of the nurses in the national hospital left for the south to set up triage facilities for the fighting. Many of us volunteered to fill in at the hospital. We collected blankets, toothbrushes, and soap; later we learned that the blankets and toothbrushes and soap were given to the rebels. Many of them had wives and children living in the camps with them.

One amazing story we heard afterward is that His Majesty had visited the camps several times over the years, and in order to get a correct tally of the number of people living there, he had his soldiers hand out apples from giant baskets they carried on their backs. After the visits the soldiers counted the leftover apples to determine how many people were in the camps.

Since he'd announced to the rebels he was coming to the main camp, and since all of his other visits had been cordial, the morning of the attack the rebels were cooking chapatis in preparation for his breakfast, so needless to say they were caught off guard. The Bhutanese army quickly overran all 30 of the camps and after a short fight, the rebels surrendered.

Here in Thimphu we donated blood and tried to go about our lives and ignore the men with guns, the Bhutanese Militia, guarding important buildings. Namgay's sister lives next door to the Royal Monetary Authority, which she said was heavily guarded. The soldiers told her and her neighbors not to let their children play on the fencing next to their house or they might accidentally get shot. The soldiers also told them to sleep with one eye open and be ready for anything.

The Food Corporation of Bhutan stockpiled food. The government asked foreigners who lived and worked in Bhutan to "take a vacation and leave the country."

If it had been a few years earlier I would have left. But now Bhutan was home. Besides, I wouldn't leave without Namgay, and even if he was allowed to leave the country, we had no immediate place to go. I started to understand why people stayed put when things got dangerous or dodgy. People want to stay with the people and things they truly love, even if it's dangerous.

Would the many Indian nationals living and working in Thimphu rise up and rebel? Were they actually rebel spies? Would the Indian Army come in and take over? What about the Chinese? Would they inject themselves into the situation? Would we run out of food? There were so many uncertainties that I had never experienced before. Fear came in and took up residence. I realized quickly that keeping to a daily routine was the best way to live with it. Just carry on.

Our borders with India were sealed. I stopped hiking above the Army base in the hills and orchards and kept close to the house. I met friends in town and had lunch, but our conversations were forced and quiet, and we had to go through a gauntlet of checkpoints to get anywhere. In his studio, Namgay painted and chanted prayers all day as usual, and he seemed almost jolly. That's the thing about pessimists. When things are dismal, they often turn cheerful. They feel validated, happy to have their worst suspicions confirmed.

I asked him if he was worried.

"No," he said.

"Why not?"

He said Guru Rinpoche, the Buddhist saint who brought Buddhism to Bhutan in the 8th century, made predictions about the future. "He said that nothing would happen to Bhutan in this century," Namgay said. "Guru predicted things wouldn't go well for the Tibetans. He got that right."

"Yes, things didn't go so well for the Tibetans," I said. After a moment I added, "But what if he's wrong? You know? What if something bad happens to Bhutan?"

Namgay thought a minute and then said, laughing, "Then it will be the end of the world."

That was something of a conversation stopper. But strangely, I found his comment comforting. The end of the world meant death, the end of life as we know it, extinction, nothingness, I'm not sure what all. But let's stop at nothing. Nothing to worry about. And I think for the first time in my life—with this very real military action going on around us, and the uncertainty of what would happen—the lack of control I had, the threat that the Army wouldn't succeed or that the fighting would reach Thimphu, made me start to think differently.

Facing the prospect of possible imminent death gave me a gateway to contemplate and confront my mortality, which was a relief. And then nothing much changed. It wasn't so bad.

Mercifully, within a couple of weeks the fighting was over. I have to say that it changed me in that, although I felt relieved and safe, I never, to this day, stopped thinking about death, giving it a nod, reflecting on it every day. It's always nearby. And also for Bhutan in a metaphorical sense there was a death of innocence.

The next spring I stood at the wall beside our house and felt the sun on my face. Cosmos grew wild there, an alien species that had colonized and taken over every-thing. The farmers hate it. But I remember lovingly culti-vating it in my garden in Tennessee. Across the river the bank was pink with it, and there were about five different shades going from hot pink to flat white. With no wind they were static pink dots among the green, up the side of the broad hill that goes for about half a kilometer from the river to the main road like the side of a bowl. The newly sprouting rice in the paddies, a beautiful kelly green the color of parrots and emeralds, was rimmed with many more cosmos. Beyond the road, miles away there were rows of low, flat Army barracks at Lungtenphu, and above that a big dark green mountain pushed up toward the blue sky that we get in the Himalayas because there's not much air and we're so close to heaven. Close to the top of the mountain, sitting among the trees, was a white monastery that, if you didn't know it was there, you would miss, as it is so high up. I remember feeling like I'd seen this view for the first time after that tough winter, but the difficulty of it and the almost daily thoughts of death, rather than making me feel depressed and gloomy, actu-ally uplifted me.

I realized thinking about death doesn't depress me. It makes me seize the moment and see things I might not ordinarily see. The beautiful view I enjoyed that spring day was even more pleasing and poignant and delightful because our lives had been difficult that winter. It had occurred to me I might not ever see it again.

My best advice: go there. Think the unthinkable, the thing that scares you to think about several times a day. Go to the outward reaches of your mind where you auto-matically avoid going. Because training yourself to think about death can give you an ease of living and a focus that will actually empower you and make you less scared. If you think about death enough, all your reactions to it—the fear, dread, terror, anxiety, hoarding stuff both mental and physical, and repugnance—eventually dissolve, like the last gasp of a candle. And then all you can do is laugh.

The Bhutanese say we should think about death at least five times a day. If you remember that we are all impermanent, it will certainly clarify things for you. Just remember that dying is the hard part. Death is probably comparatively easy.

SIMPLE IS GENIUS

When I think of simplifying my life, I think of nutcrackers.

In March 2000, the auspicious Year of the Dragon, I married Namgay. In November, with eight solid months of marriage under our belts, we traveled to India, Thailand, and finally to the U.S. It was my first time out of Bhutan in more than three years. Namgay had traveled in Asia but had never been to the U.S.

It seemed like a lifetime since I'd left my ancestral home, not to mention the rest of the planet, for the magical land of Bhutan. We planned to travel around, see friends and some of the geographical splendor of North America, and celebrate our marriage in Nashville.

The week before our epic journey, we went to a Black-necked Crane festival near the school in Phobjikha in central Bhutan. There's so much to love in Bhutan and there's always a celebration. That's all there is, really. It's like living in a musical. At the end of the festival, when all the villagers were still sitting beside the school, not wanting to leave, some of them got up and started singing and dancing.

If people are dancing, I'll join in. We danced all night around an enormous bonfire; the stars were so bright and close it seemed like we could reach out and grab them.

It was hard to leave only a few days later. We hopped from New Delhi, to Bangkok, to Tokyo, to Detroit, to Atlanta and were scooped up at the airport in Nashville to join a whirlwind of activities we were the center of— parties, visits with friends, movies, dinners, and more. We kept going and going and going, but I can't remember any dancing.

I do remember a lot of shopping, which was, to my mind, equally as magical as the stars in Phobjikha Valley. In 2000 there was a lot of wonderful stuff in the stores and everyone was shopping like nobody's business.

It took no time for Namgay to figure out that "coupons" are a thing, that merchandise in the stores goes on sale with some regularity (as opposed to Bhutan, where it never does), that everything is for sale, and that everything is a few dollars cheaper if you drive down the road a little bit or look online.

If you can't sleep and are jet-lagged, you can go to the grocery store because it never closes, except on Christmas Day and maybe Thanksgiving. If you don't want to leave home, just turn on the television and shop, or watch as merchandise is paraded on the screen and listen while other people shop and talk about it and pay in three easy installments.

It was fun to look at things with Namgay. I saw them in a different light and I knew the sheer excess of it all blew his mind, rewired his synapses, and opened a whole new world to him. He'd never been a visitor in the land of plenty. Spray paint, which he'd never seen before, became an obsession. He spray-painted my parents' wrought-iron lawn furniture and a lot of other stuff until we made him stop.

He didn't want much, but what he wanted was of very nice quality. He has an artist's eye for good workmanship and quality fabrics.

"Do you want that sweater?" I'd ask, watching him test its seams.

"We'll wait for it to go on sale," he'd say with a knowing look, putting it under a stack of similar sweaters. He'd been schooled by my aunt, an excellent bargain shopper.

The after-Christmas sales put us over the top weight-wise. That is to say we kept filling up suitcases to take back to Bhutan and we joked about leasing a big cargo plane, but it would be too big to fly into Paro airport. That was the golden age of cramming, and airlines were way more lenient about things like weight and size, and if you went a few pounds or a few inches over the limit, then they would let it go. And we did crazy things like carry large bottles of liquids in our carry-ons.

It was such a wild collection of things. I took a set of Calphalon pots; Namgay packed a compound bow; we had a small vacuum. Oh, the things, the things! We packed shoes and clothes for everyone we knew in Bhutan. We packed coats, food, toothbrushes, and books. Nothing was too heavy or insignificant for us to purchase and pack. We'd look at each other after seeing this or that car, or a steaming device for clothing, or a clothes dryer, and say wistfully, "I wish we could have that in Bhutan." If we could have packed up a chunk of the U.S. and schlepped it to Bhutan we would have. It was like we'd never seen any of the stuff before, which in Namgay's case was true. Namgay fell in love with a popcorn machine on wheels, convinced it would make him a multimillionaire if he could get it to Bhutan. But then he did some math and abandoned the idea. We packed two coffeepots and a meat grinder made of iron as consolation.

To say we went overboard is to grossly understate the situation.

People gave us wedding gifts and we had a stack of gift cards. We had no idea what these were until somebody told us the gift cards would allow us to shop more! And we didn't have to pay! Just give the store one of these cards! In Bhutan if you said, "Let me see your card," the person would pull out his citizenship card. It is still refreshingly free of credit cards, gift cards, and membership cards. The entire inventory of things you can buy in Thimphu would not fill one half of one Walmart superstore.

Near the end of our shopping orgy I found a nutcracker at Williams-Sonoma and we had the aforementioned gift cards, so I said I wanted it. It was shaped like pliers—a nice, serviceable, simple design.

Namgay said we didn't need a nutcracker. "But we have those really nice walnuts in Bhutan," I said. Who knows why I chose the nutcracker at Williams-Sonoma to take a stand over? We were tired, we'd had a long afternoon at the mall, and Namgay had just spent a grueling session at Restoration Hardware getting flashlights, maps, key rings, hammers, compasses, and solar radios for the entire population of Bhutan.

Maybe that's why I insisted on it and I might even have made a pouty face or squirted tears, and so I got the nutcracker. It was a little bit heavy, but just a drop in the bucket considering what we'd already bought.

A friend in Nashville says she thinks people like to talk about simplifying their lives, and they like to think about simplifying their lives, but most don't want to go there. They go to the Container Store instead and load up on more things to put their stuff in. I agree to a point. I'd take it further and say that it really doesn't matter what we *want*. All of us, at some point in our lives, will be forced by the universe, or finances, or sanity, or fire, or society, or by sickness or natural disaster, or whatever circumstances, to pare down. It could be because we move or divorce, or it could be economic. And then there's the ultimate "pare down" when we go to that big yard sale in the sky. Guess what we won't take with us? Everything. But less doesn't mean less quality of life. That is clear to me now.

The need to simplify will most likely be because of a lack of resources. That's how it happened for me when I moved to Bhutan. There was a drastic difference in what I could get in Bhutan and what I lived with in the U.S. It wasn't bad, either. In fact, it was good. Benefits of simplifying are that you live more in the moment, you use less, you depend on friends and family more, there's less to dust and insure, and you dance more. It opens physical and mental space in your life. You like yourself more. It's like taking a big emotional poop.

I've given away or given up or sold or lost whole households, freighters full of books, furniture, old magazines, junk mail, used bottles, used assorted paper, furniture, jewelry, appliances. I am one of seven billion people on the planet, a speck on the surface of the earth, and look what's gone through my fingers. I remember things fondly: my grandmother's enormous smoky topaz rings, my black-and-white trompe-l'oeil table, my beautiful kiln rugs, thousands of books. So much in my life has relocated and left me. I want to remember the stuff, but I want to care less about what I have or don't have.

A Scandinavian friend who worked at the UN said she was invited to dinner by a co-worker in New Delhi. She took a taxi to the area where her friend said she lived, and her friend was there and led her to a cardboard hut on the side of the road, where she and her family lived. She worked for the UN in New Delhi and she was homeless and squatting by the side of the road. The evening was great, by the way.

What's really interesting is that I told the story to an American friend and she just flat-out said she didn't believe me.

Believe me, people in the world live with much less and in pretty appalling (to us) circumstances. But they survive and even thrive.

Even with the aforementioned leniency, we paid $800 in overweight fees to Delta to get back to Bhutan, and I have conveniently forgotten what we paid Drukair to haul our swag. It was a lot of money for us, not to mention it was mentally taxing. It was like traveling with a whole other person—a fat person with no brain or muscles and a lot of heft.

When we finally got back to Thimphu the vacuum cleaner quit the second time we used it. The mixer overheated and died in the service of making meringue. (Did you know you can freeze meringue?) And the nutcracker fell apart in my hands three days after we got home.

Namgay and I were in the kitchen when it happened and he said, "Wait!" and ran outside. He came back carrying a smooth gray river rock. "Watch!" he said, and leveraged the rock so it hit the walnut in just the right place. The shell cracked in two and the nut slid out whole. He handed it to me, smiling.

Months of traveling during that first U.S. visit took us to Florida to see my brother and his family. My sister went along with us and talked as she drove. I sat next to her in front; Namgay sat in back. Her mother-in-law, Ruby, known to her grandchildren as Mima, had sold her house in Alabama, and my sister, along with the rest of the family, had been busy helping to disperse and store 60 years of belongings. Mima and her husband, now deceased, had raised three children in the house. As she drove, my sister kept up a steady monologue about various people and relatives I hadn't thought of in years . . .

"Mary Grace did Princeton this summer. Kept calling while we were packing up Mima's house. Said she had to read seven hundred fifty pages a night. Fell asleep on the stairs of her dorm coming home from class. Crying because she wouldn't see Mima's house again. We all had to cry because Mary Grace wouldn't see Mima's house again."

We crested a hill on Highway 286 at Grant, Alabama. One of those signs on wheels sat in front of a white cinderblock church. It said, THE BEST VITAMIN FOR A CHRISTIAN IS B-1!

I turned around to see if Namgay was taking in my sister's monologue featuring sentences with no subjects. He was gazing out the window, lips moving, silently chanting prayers.

We liked the beach and ocean in Florida, but the flatness was oppressive. He hated the way American families rarely gathered together and said things like, "So how is your life?" and were always on the go.

We flew to Denver and got a shuttle to Boulder. Namgay said, "I don't ever want to go back to Florida."

"That can be arranged," I said.

We waited in the back of a minibus for 30 minutes for someone to show up and help an overweight dwarf woman in a wheelchair at the curb board the bus. I was worried about all our suitcases and whether they'd make it to Bhutan. I felt preoccupied and weighed down.

The woman in the wheelchair made it into the front seat of the van. It was 101 degrees that day, and she said it was hotter in Denver than in Orlando, where she was from. That's how we all knew she was from Orlando. A tour guide, an elderly man, led the conversation for all of us in the back of the bus, and agreed it was "hotter than a pistol." He was dapper, in a Panama hat and sunglasses, but on closer inspection he was elderly and frail with dyed black hair and a fake tan. He reminded me of the protagonist of Thomas Mann's *Death in Venice*, a distinguished German gentleman at the turn of the century who, in an attempt to regain his youth, succumbs to the fashion of the day in Italy, dying his hair black and wearing makeup and bright red lipstick that only makes him look grotesque and sad. The famous actor Dirk Bogarde played him in a movie of the same name in 1971.

They had a conversation about extreme weather conditions they had endured, trying to one-up each other, and then Dirk Bogarde mentioned the big palmetto bugs— flying roaches that can get as big as four inches long. Definitely another downside of Florida.

"When I was stationed in the Army . . ." he began, but I officially quit listening as I have heard many variations of that palmetto bug story. Besides, I needed to concentrate on worrying about the luggage and whether the glass bowl I had foolishly packed in our duffel would make it without breaking.

We were changing planes at the airport in St. Louis and had a very short time to get off the plane, get boarding passes, and make our connecting flight. I was sad to be leaving, thinking it might be the last time I saw some of the people I loved. But I was also happy to be going back to Bhutan. The frenzy of life on the road, staying in hotels, being in transit or houseguests for months, made me frazzled.

Waiting in line to check in, an elderly woman in a sari, who looked Indian, struggled mightily with an enormous suitcase, trying to negotiate the few feet from the check-in desk over to a security kiosk. She looked tired and drained, struggling to keep her dignity, weighed down by her possessions.

I understood her plight. We are always so weighted down by things—mainly gifts, requests from friends, things we think we need, necessities for friends and family, and things we like but don't really need.

Everyone in the long line stood passively, holding or standing by their own bags, watching the woman as she fought with the big immigrant suitcase. Suddenly the thing we all fear happened: the zipper gave way. The bag popped open and her stuff spilled out. People's stuff looks so ratty when suitcases burst open.

Namgay deftly stepped over the rope barriers and grabbed each side of the bag, minimizing the fallout. He helped her tie her large dupatta shawl and a pashmina around it, knotting the ends ingeniously so they fit the suitcase like a sleeve. Then they lifted it off the ground together and put it on the conveyor. She staggered slightly, adjusting to the absence of weight. He caught her by the elbow. Then he came back and stood beside me in line.

It was a moment of clarity. She was one of us, more so than my own family—a migrant, struggling to transit through airports to get to the other side of the world and hauling a bunch of useless things. It made me cry. And I cried until our plane took off from St. Louis.

Later, as the plane rose above Seattle and then over the mountains and into the clouds, I was suddenly comforted by the prospect of many hours of flight over the milky ocean. Hours of calm. Hours of nothing.

It's so true. A rock makes an excellent nutcracker.

LOOK FOR MAGIC

I've always thought that for magic to work you have to be lost; you have to lose control. I don't mean the tiresome sleight-of-hand magic that Las Vegas magicians do. I mean real, out-and-out magic that happens around us but we're too busy to notice. I've also thought that our constant connections to machines, computers, phones, pads, and such make it difficult for us in the West to see magic, to get in touch with our sense of wonder, to be amazed. But I've revised this a bit, as you will see.

How many times in the last month have you had a sense of wonder, like constructing-a-miniature-mountain-from-mashed-potatoes wonder, something that compelled you to get up out of your chair and go look out the window and stand gape-mouthed, astonished? It just doesn't happen that often. But we're programmed to want it. We want something to amaze us. That's why YouTube works, and carnivals, and big-budget action movies. It's why people go around saying, "That's amazing!" about things that aren't really. We have to hone our awareness and look for magic. And that's why I feel like we have to get lost, or rather, we have to change our perception of reality to find magic. Living with Namgay in the U.S., I've revised everything I think about reality and magic. Now I think magic happens all the time.

Here's how it is: Namgay and I are in the U.S. and I'm watching television and he comes in and sits down. Maybe there's a car chase where the hero or someone is driving a car and he loses control and the car careens over a cliff. It lands upside down and bursts into flames. Namgay will say, "Is this real?"

I know what he's asking. He's wondering if he's walked in on a documentary about Toyotas with locking gas pedals, or a car chase caught live, à la O.J., filmed from a local news helicopter, or maybe it's a movie. He's smart, but he didn't grow up watching American television— or any television—and he doesn't take anything at face value, because he's in a strange new culture. He just needs clarification.

"It's not real. It's a movie," I say.

Likewise, when we're watching the news, he'll often ask, "Is this real?"

Again, it's an idle question, habitual, and I like it when he asks, but sometimes I'm not sure what to answer, or I start to qualify my answers. "Yes. This is *very* real," I say, watching thousands of Egyptians flood Tahrir Square, and fire and bombs and shooting. It's the horror of civil war.

He flips the channel to a reality show where two people are arguing, or someone is crying, or sitting pensively on a bed. "Is this real?"

"It's sort of real," I say. I start to feel like an umpire making a call during a baseball game. I revise my call. "No. Actually it's not real," I say.

When we were first getting to know each other long ago, he asked me about my education.

"I have an MFA in fiction," I said.

"What's fiction?" he asked.

How cool is it that he didn't understand the concept of fiction? That's why I married him. No, not really.

"Fiction is stuff you make up. Stories that aren't real."

"What do you mean?"

"You know, when you tell a story and you make up characters and you have them do things like fly around in the air or maybe there's a dragon in it."

He looked at me blankly. I decided to drop it.

What is real? What is magical? It's magical to be able to move between the Himalayan culture of Bhutan and the American South with Namgay. It kind of ramps up the fascination factor in both places.

Once we were at a party, a rather large gathering, and it was when we'd first married and we were spending a few months in the U.S. Namgay and I were standing in the garden of this lovely house where the party was held, and a beautiful older woman wearing a pink chiffon dress and a big matching hat came up to me and said all in one delicious, Southern-drawled, cracked-out sentence: "I know you; I know your family; I grew up with your mother; who ARE you?"

I looked at Namgay beside me. "I'm Linda Leaming," I said. "You knew my mother, Dorothy. This is my husband . . . Namgay."

"Well, Linda! How are you?" She looked at Namgay. "Hello, Man-GAY," she said, smiling broadly and seemingly oblivious to the fact that she'd butchered his name in a semi-accusatory, outing, but nonetheless amusing way. "Isn't this the most beautiful garden you have ever seen?"

He smiled but couldn't bring himself to speak. He wasn't fluent in Southern.

"It is just spectacular," I said, letting every bit of my Southernness ooze out of my mouth. "And isn't the ham heavenly?" The ham wasn't really heavenly; I just wanted to say something alliterative.

People don't talk like that in Bhutan. I half expected Namgay to lean over to me and say, "Is this real?" I'm not sure which side I'd come down on.

What Namgay thinks is magical are electric drills, self-serve soft-swirl ice cream that's free with a meal, salad spinners, anything made by Ronco, Cinnabon sweet rolls, coupons, buying pants and getting a free alteration, American grocery stores, tape measures, toilets that flush unaided, debit cards, and leaf blowers.

Real? Magical? Unreal? Fantastic? Weird? I'm not sure what these words mean anymore. Seeing the world through Namgay's eyes turns my world on its head. When we first came to the U.S. we lived in rural Tennessee for a few months. It helped us to avoid a crash landing in a larger city and to adapt slowly, like putting your toes in really cold water and then easing the rest of your body in. There were small towns all around, and corn, tobacco, and cows. It was American living lite—plenty of space around but only a few people to deal with, and not that much to absorb but Mother Nature. There were a lot of Amish nearby and the subsequent Amish groceries, bakeries, lumberyards, and quilting concerns. Namgay didn't trust the Amish. He thought they weren't real. He couldn't get behind the idea that their faith dictated not using electricity, motorized vehicles, or zippers. In the holy land of consumerism, the richest, most technologically advanced country in the world, they wouldn't use any of it. He didn't find it magical at all. Once I insisted we stop to look at some Amish quilts and Namgay said that as we drove up, a little Amish girl ran into the house, kicked off her shoes, and came outside barefoot. I cannot confirm this.

In the early evenings we'd take walks along the country lanes that lined the perimeters of nearby farms. The cows would stop and stare; whole herds looked stunned as we walked by. With mouthfuls of grass they stopped chewing as if we were aliens, unaccustomed to people who weren't bringing them feed or opening and closing gates.

It had been ten years or more since I'd seen Tennessee wildflowers and I loved to look on the sides of the road—cedum, pink and purple thistle blooms, Queen Anne's lace, Astor daisies, that rich sweet smell of honeysuckle, all brought back memories.

I told Namgay over 80 percent of all flowers are white. He was unimpressed. He was impressed with farm equipment, however: big green John Deere combines and bush hoggers that one of our neighbors used to let him drive. Namgay was in hog heaven.

He said the terrain looked like India. I knew he was trying to get a feel for where he was, some point of reference. Compared to mountainous Bhutan, I guess Tennessee does look like parts of India. India has plenty of farmland, but it's shabby and brown compared to the rolling farms and lush fields of Tennessee. Bhutan's farms are postage stamps, terraced up the sides of steep mountains. The poor cows have only the sides of the narrow mountain roads to forage for spindly grass and scrub. Everything is closed in, a tiny world crisscrossed by slender mountain roads and trails, where bears and tigers roam, and a mountain mist can sneak in and shroud anything and look like dragon's breath.

"Tennessee is nothing like India," he said a few weeks later on one of our evening walks.

He liked looking at the sky and the white vapor trails the jets made. No planes fly over Bhutan, so jets fascinated him. Anything in the sky does. In the afternoons he could count five or six when I was still looking for the first one. Some were so high up they were nearly impossible to see, faint dots with etched lines high up in the stratosphere.

"I like it that people are up there," he said. "They're in the plane and they're drinking tea. They're going to the toilet and shitting!"

What an alarming thought. I looked at the tiny speck of a plane and thought of airplane toilets. Years of flying coach on long-distance flights and using the ever-shrinking lavatories have made me a germaphobe. It's dreadful to even think about them—their sickly antiseptic smell that doesn't quite mask, but mixes unpleasantly with, other smells; the litter, the way people are so careless and don't clean up after themselves; the gooey, sticky floor after twelve hours over the Pacific; the alarming noise the vacuum makes when you flush and the bowl evacuates. I could go on but I will spare you. The plane was a tiny cursor in the air, trailing a white tail. And there were people in it. And yes, there were people in those toilets.

"It's magic," I said.

"I know," he said.

The fact that Namgay and I have stayed together, even thrived, for so long, is pretty magical. I think miracles happen and we're too busy to notice. In the West we've gained wonderful things like wealth and efficiency, but I think we've lost a great deal of instinct, perception, sixth sense, insight, call it what you like. But when you're occupied every minute of the day with surviving, there's simply no time for these things. We are all, in our own way, like the subsistence farmers of Bhutan, just trying to keep our heads above water.

But in one way Bhutan is different. Magic, mystery, miracles, and the supernatural are part of the history of the place. Padmasambhava, or Guru Rinpoche, the Buddhist saint who brought Buddhism to Bhutan in the 8th century, flew on the back of a tiger to a cliff face and built Taktsang. You can still see it today and I challenge you to not look at it, or even to go there and not have a sense of amazement for the sheer gravity-defying, solid-mass-floating-on-air aspect of it. It is truly a wonder. I'm always amazed when I go up and come down in one piece and don't fall off one of the many sheer rock faces you have to traverse to get there.

And what about these dragons, anyway? Nobody in Bhutan will say definitively they've ever seen one, but once I was talking with a friend in the market and I told him I was writing a book. There was a sudden, loud thunderclap. My friend in all seriousness said, "The dragon approves!"

One day when he was young Namgay came home from school and told his mother Americans walked on the moon.

"Who is walking on the moon?"

"Americans."

"Who?"

"Americans. People with cars that can go to the moon."

"Ahhhhhh! *Go na!*" She raised her hand threatening to rap him on the head with her knuckle. "Don't lie!"

"*Shapjapne me!*" (I'm not lying!) "Teacher said it."

Later, in the U.S., we visited the Space and Rocket Center in Huntsville, Alabama, and Namgay had a magical moment of validation seeing moon rocks and the actual spaceship that went to the moon. He started painting American rockets, specifically Apollo 13 rockets, and incorporating his Bhutanese iconography. Thirteen is his lucky number. He said American rockets are like Bhutanese dragons. And sometimes in the U.S. he feels like he's isolated, all alone, riding off somewhere really fast, and he has no idea where he's going. The paintings are magical, by the way.

To marry a Bhutanese thangka painter is fairy-tale-like, and even kind of crazy, which is a less polite word for magical. Truthfully, intercultural marriage is a slog, but magic is right there in the mundane. I think of being nine years old in elementary school in the solidly middle-class American suburbs of Nashville. I gained a rudimentary knowledge of the world via social studies and *Weekly Readers*. I loved to read fairy tales about dragons and knights and to go swimming and to visit the mall with my friends. I knew I wanted to see the world, and I knew instinctively that my life would take many turns. I was sure I would have adventure.

When Namgay was nine, he walked about a month, barefoot, from his family's home in Trongsa in the middle of the Himalayas. There was no road. He went with his uncle, a Buddhist holy man in long, red robes, to the edge of their known world of Lhuntse in remote Eastern Bhutan. Namgay learned *Choekay*, the Tibetan religious language, and studied obscure Buddhist scriptures sitting on a wooden plank in the trees above a small corn patch in a clearing in the woods. He learned to outsmart monkeys and survive on plants in the forest. His world was a spiritual realm inside his own head. Twenty-six years later, neither of us having changed very much, we married. I still wake up every morning and think that's enchantment enough for a lifetime.

Believing that there is more to life than the clinical, the mundane, and the political has taken on real importance as I get older. I need to believe that there are unexplainable things, and that not everything can be picked apart through painstaking deconstruction.

Believe in magic and you might not experience magic, but you might experience something close to it, or something equally wonderful. Dresden China was discovered in 17th-century Germany when the alchemist Johann Friedrich Böttger was conscripted by the Saxon king to try to make gold. So there you are.

A few years ago, we introduced Namgay's mother to Skype. We were in the U.S. and she was in Bhutan. We said hello and she said *"Kuzu!"* (Hello!) We all laughed a solid three minutes just looking at each other. We couldn't stop. And then she got up and walked around behind the computer. *"Ane terribarri?"* (Is this real?) she said.

I don't think all that much is real. But I see magic everywhere.

SEE THE
WORLD WITH
YOUR HEART

"Eden exists, we just choose not to look for it," said my friend, the photographer, author, and explorer John Guider. There are some of us who make it our life's work to look for beauty, to see the world. By seeing the world, I mean to look under the skirts of whatever's going on, to suss out meaning, to figure things out and get at all the angles to find the subtext.

From traveling from one end of the earth to the other and from living in obscure places, I think I've figured out how the world works and how to see it.

See the world with your heart.

Sometimes when we arrive in the U.S. or in Bhutan it feels like we've been shot out of a cannon, because travel these days is rigorous and aerobic. It's also confusing. Once we'd been in New Delhi for a few weeks and then we landed in Tennessee. We decided we would drive to

Nashville and go to a movie in one of the malls. I noticed Namgay sitting at the desk before we left, poring over a map. He kept saying, "Where is it? I can't find it!"

"Where's what?" I asked.

"The Pria Center," he said. "I can't find it on a map."

"The Pria Center is a shopping mall in New Delhi," I said. "Remember? We're going to Green Hills Mall in Nashville."

Also he was looking at a map of Kentucky.

There's abundant wildlife in middle Tennessee, and our front yard seems to be part of a migration route for animals of all kinds: deer, turkey, fox, heron, skunks, and lots of snakes. One morning during breakfast Namgay pointed out a groundhog standing in our side yard in front of the woods that border the property. The groundhog was maybe 20 feet away from our kitchen window. Namgay said he came out every morning for breakfast. If I had sat there for a hundred years and looked outside, I never would have seen him, because he was nicely camouflaged and I'm not predisposed to look. But Namgay's eyes, trained from birth to focus on the natural world, saw the groundhog with no problem. It became part of my day to look for him, and most every morning I bothered to look, the groundhog would eventually show up; animals are creatures of habit. He'd stand on his hind legs and sniff up at the sun or forage in the grass, stuffing himself so he could go to sleep for the winter. He looked disheveled and a little beat-up. He reminded me of Christopher Hitchens.

We spent the next year in Bhutan and then came back to Tennessee. The groundhog had been busy while we were away, and instead of his solitary bachelor life, now he had a wife and three babies. In the spring, Namgay had a commission and was leaving for a month to go work

at a temple. When I drove back from taking him to the airport I saw one of the babies dead in the road, hit by a car. I wondered which of the babies it was, and I couldn't shake the sadness all day. That's what happens when you see the world. The world is so painful sometimes.

Our place in Tennessee had a small army of locals who kept it immaculate. I used to love it when Janey and Trina came to clean the house because they were hugely entertaining. Janey, smiling and kindly with gray hair, moved slowly and methodically as she cleaned the floors, vacuumed, and mopped. Trina, short and wiry, with red hair and enough energy for both of them, liked to do things like climb ladders to dust the ceiling fans, put new shelf paper in the cabinets, and clean the oven. They often had a steady stream of conversation going about anything and everything, and I always liked being around them. I'm from a tradition of big talkers and storytellers. The Bhutanese are also storytellers, but I love the familiar cadence and stories of these Southern ladies and I realize it was one of the things I missed most living in Bhutan. It's like a verbal swarm of bees.

We'd just arrived back in the U.S. from Bhutan and Janey asked me when I was in the U.S. last. I told her I came three years before, when my mother died.

"I'm so sorry," Janey said.

"She had cancer," I said.

I had only to say the word *cancer* and they were off—Janey, leaning on a mop and speaking with her soft, slow enunciation and open, unguarded face, and Trina with her quick Southern twang, up on a ladder attacking a light fixture with what looked to be a toothbrush and a squirt bottle. Change languages and situations and it could be a conversation among three women in a village in Bhutan.

Trina said to Janey, "You know that woman over on Old Quest Road? You know she has liver cancer and they quit treating her last week. Say they can't do any more. She doesn't have any family. I clean her house every week and I've been taking her to the doctor on Tuesdays."

"Old Quest or New Quest?" Janey said.

"You know. Her name's Richards but she's not kin to any of the Richards there in Coopertown. She's the one without any family. I'm helping her sort through her stuff. She wants to get rid of all her old magazines."

"Those Richards have the farm over there by the new school."

"She's got that white house near where they had that accident."

"Oh yeah," Janey said. "I know her. What's she going to do with the magazines?"

"I cart them over to the senior citizens' center."

"Have you eaten at that restaurant over there by the center?"

"Which one?"

"That one that has that fudge pie with the mint ice cream."

"I have a good recipe for fudge pie," I said, injecting myself into the conversation, trying to divert it just for fun.

"We went there with Jerry and them," Trina said, stepping off the ladder and grabbing a bag of trash. "I want that recipe," she added on her way out the door.

It's the same in Bhutan; a disease (cancer, diabetes— any malady, really) is a good conversation starter any- where in the world. But the conversation will probably take off on a wild roller coaster into parts unknown. What I understand is people all over the world are not that different. We're the same in our hearts and we can make connections with people even if we don't speak the same language. Connections can come from any random thing.

Namgay and an elderly friend in Nashville have a connection because they both like to watch *The Apprentice* on TV. They hardly speak to each other. But they have this connection and watch it together.

There is a place so foreign to me and so remote from anyplace I know, but when I go there I have an instant connection and I always have a sort of longing to be there. I don't completely understand why, but it gets me in my heart. It's the part of India below Bhutan, the Duars Plains, and the Himalayan foothills to the west with the lively, crowded towns of Kalimpong and Darjeeling, with buildings perched impossibly on the sides of hills. And Kanchenjunga—at over 28,000 feet, the third-highest mountain in the world—sits like a majestic protector, which is what the locals believe it to be. The Teesta River winds down the mountains, which are covered with thick forests, and it widens a bit as it curves through the plains. Even its name, *Teesta*, evokes a flicker of tenderness inside me. On the map, the Indian state of West Bengal is a slivery geopolitical doodle that connects Calcutta, now Kolkata, and the Indian Ocean in the south with the Himalayas in the north. Up around Bhutan the foothills of Darjeeling comprise farmland and tea plantations. West Bengal is minuscule land-wise, but officially it contains 90 million people, one of the most densely populated states in India. Unofficially, who knows how many people are there. There are 17 million or so undocumented Nepalese, pushed out of their homeland, living without rights or country in that part of Northeast India. Its rolling hills are parched and overworked and swarming with souls—a mass of people, goats, cows, cars, dust, noise, and dogs. I think of India in a brown haze, and in comparison, Tennessee looks voluptuous, green, and rich; rolling hills with hardwoods that grow poetically in clumps in the middle of fields. In India there is so much struggle to survive. And that particular part of India is a forgotten part of the world. There is enormous energy there. Everyone appears to be hauling gargantuan loads of grass, wood, or palm fronds on foot, or on bicycles, pulling loads on carts, feeding animals. The people are lean, leathery skeletons with black eyes and faces that show the hardness of their lives. The only things that flow and have color are the graceful saris the women wear. Everyone is working as hard as they possibly can. Life is an enormous struggle. People are at a level of survival. I suppose I feel the connection in my heart because I'm also a survivor. When I see a poor woman holding her child it reminds me we're all in our own way enduring, carrying on. I feel this so strongly in India.

We are all, on some level, survivors.

The landscape is so vast, and the trees are deformed and overworked, their lower limbs poached for firewood. Every bit of earth is used and ancient, planted or settled with a house or a dirt road, a cultivated field, a temple, a building plastered with signs. Everything has a not-unpleasant, used, askew look—worn-out, and dusty.

During our last trip to Darjeeling, a bridge had washed out at Binnaguri in the flat part where tea plantations and jute farms dominate the landscape. For more than a mile, there were trucks parked on the side of the road, and makeshift kitchens with open-air fires had popped up to cook food and sell it to the truckers. Someone told our driver they had been there for three days. We opted to take a detour through some remote villages and farms on one-lane dirt roads. It was market day, and everyone was bringing jute to market to sell. There were masses of coiled brown jute everywhere: jute draped over the sides of bridges to dry, jute being twisted into rope by men and women, enormous jute loads coiled and carried on the backs of bicycles or pushed on carts. Sometimes the piles on the carts were over eight feet high and beautiful young girls in bright saris sat on the very tops of the loads like little goddesses.

At one point the road passed through a marshy area with water on each side, the dirt road slightly elevated. Gangs of young men with homemade "receipt books" had fashioned a makeshift tollgate to extort money for cars passing through the village. They probably belonged to one of the hundreds of antigovernment organizations that want to secede from India and revert Bengal to a sovereign country. Good luck with that. Our Indian driver got angry and refused to pay. They let us go. Later we made it back on the main road and passed two male dogs mounting a female dog at the same time as if to emphasize even more the coarseness of life.

A week later on the way back to Thimphu, we were happy to find the bridge fixed, so we didn't have to make the detour. We were only an hour or so from the Bhutanese border when we saw what looked to be an elephant with a large crowd of people standing around it ahead on the side of the road. As we got closer it was clear that there had been an accident. It was an Army truck, not an elephant;

it had gone off the road and landed on its side in a ditch. I saw the remnants of a badly mangled motorcycle under its left rear wheel. I didn't see the driver of the motorcycle, but the angry mob of dozens of young men shouting and gesturing beside the truck surrounded a lone Army officer in a red beret and Indian Army uniform. He must have been the driver of the truck. He was a good-looking man, tall and thin with a movie star's chiseled looks, and our car passed close enough so that I was able to see the look of supreme sorrow on his face. He raised his right arm in the air above his head, his hand formed into a fist, and he put his head down. I don't know what the gesture meant, but it was devastating to see.

I asked Namgay if we should stop or try to do something, but it was our driver who answered. He said no, we had to keep going. "If we stop, only God knows what may happen to us."

"What will happen? Will he be okay?" Nobody answered me. It's not uncommon in this part of India for mobs to take the law into their own hands and stone or kick perceived wrongdoers to death.

It seemed like I didn't breathe until we passed through the Bhutan Gates in Phuentsholing. I was never so happy to be home. I couldn't stop thinking about the accident and the Army officer. A few days later I called my friend Maria in Sikkim, the Indian state above West Bengal in the Himalayas. I told her about the accident and the gesture, his fist in the air.

"Maybe it was some kind of political gesture," she said. West Bengal had been a communist state before the current government. "Maybe he was showing solidarity."

That made sense. "Do you think he's okay?" I asked, knowing there was no way she could say definitively.

"Yes," she said emphatically. "Anyway," she added, "if he's Army he'd have a gun."

"I love you for making me believe you," I said. "I don't know why I can't stop thinking about it."

"It's upsetting, and painful," she said. "That's why."

Maybe it's connected to the struggle that pulls at my heart, the toiling and slogging. There is so much effort in this part of the world. Life is fragile, stripped down to primitive, aboriginal striving. People are left to their wits and their own devices. Life is cheap. Myth gets caught up in reality, which is the way of most of the world. So this is the thing that fills me with hope and love and something like happiness: No human being can be apart from all of us. John Donne was right. "No man is an island." We are all in it together and we have to see the world. This is huge.

CHECK YOUR EGO

Much of what we do or think comes from being led by our egos, and so many conflicts happen because of our overweening desire to put ourselves first. In our self-absorption, we're conditioned to think that the world revolves around us and our needs. We are slaves to our selfhood. It's the human condition. We have to show the world we exist; we have to show what we can do. And this brings suffering. We are not, each of us, the center of the universe. The more we can walk in others' shoes and get out of our skin, the happier we will be.

Our propensity to try to dominate and outdo each other, our habit of thinking of ourselves above all causes conflict. It's what's wrong with the world. Excessive ego makes us rash, irresponsible, power grabbing, and thoughtless, and it makes us unhappy. We all have ego. And the idea isn't to get rid of it; you can't. You can subjugate it and try to ignore it, but that doesn't work ultimately, and it will rise up and everything will be even stronger and more aggressive than before. I mean that we all have problems in life that are, well, the result of living. They're caused by money, relationships, jobs, and simply negotiating life. They will always be with us and we can deal with them, but when our egos get involved, then our problems become "us." What we do is who we are—or worse, what we aspire to be. That's ego messing everything up. What we want to do is transcend ego.

Who am I? I'm not a collection of my attributes and habits. I don't need to prove my uniqueness to the world. That's a trap. We are more than our egos.

To show you how ego makes us unhappy and unintelligent I will give you an example from my own life. I will tell you a deep dark secret about my marriage: we fight. Now I'll give you a moment to absorb this because I know it's shocking. Most of our fights are ridiculous for many reasons, but mostly because of ego. For one thing we have this cultural chasm, which won't ever go away. It's in our DNA. That is to say, we're human beings.

One of the first things I did when we married was to equip myself with a pretty serviceable vocabulary for arguing in Dzongkha, Namgay's language. *"Ca che BE!"* (Why!) *"Le shim men du."* (This sucks.) *"Jeda!"* [REDACTED] *"Cheu sage!"* (You're an idiot!) It was a good idea because when we fought he heard me. And it was showing him a little respect.

Please don't be fooled by my husband's seemingly gentle demeanor and unaffected manner. He is a cold, calculating Buddhist, and believe me, he uses everything in the Buddhist arsenal: humor, truth, compassion, and a lot of other stuff that seems positive and uplifting but is actually very dark and wicked when we argue.

What do we argue about? Stupid things. Time, mostly. Namgay suffers from a malaise that afflicts many Bhutanese: he lacks the genetic coding that makes it possible to see the minute hand of a watch or clock. It makes me crazy even after all these years. Here's an example: I ask him the time. He says, "Nine o'clock." I go in the bedroom to get something and see the alarm clock. It says 9:48. When I point out his inaccuracy, that's it's really closer to ten o'clock and for all practical purposes it *is* ten o'clock, he is genuinely puzzled. He thinks I'm splitting hairs. Maybe so. To him it's nine o'clock—give or take 48 minutes. Sometimes he is accurate to the minute, such as when I ask him if he thinks it will rain. Having grown up in Bhutan, he's a man of the earth; all Bhutanese have a connection to these mountains. He's one with the elements and at peace with all sentient beings, and he can literally smell the weather. If I'm going into Thimphu proper, he'll say, "Take the umbrella. It's going to rain today." "About when?" I ask, going back inside to change into waterproof shoes. "About two thirty," he answers, and he's usually right.

This time thing gives us the most opportunities for conflict. Say we are going to a dinner or a movie, and it starts at 7:30. "We need to leave at seven," I'll say. "So get in the shower around six thirty."

At 6:50 I'll hear a buzzing sound outside and he'll be leaf blowing the driveway. I'll run outside like the time cop I am. "What are you doing? We have to leave in ten minutes!"

"It's going to rain tomorrow and the leaves will stick to the driveway. They won't blow if they're wet." Buzz. Buzz. Buzz.

"And?"

"They were getting deep."

"Namgay, there were approximately five leaves on the driveway."

"They look messy."

Okay, he is obsessive-compulsive, but this is the reason he can paint like he does. And I have to admit our driveway and yard are seriously manicured. You can tell someone with OCD lives here; they always look great.

"You live in an alternate universe! You make me responsible for scheduling you!" (See what I did there?) "I can't believe you're not ready," I say, completely believing it, even having expected it.

"I just had to blow the leaves off the driveway," he said. And then, "I give you so many problems. You're right. I am very bad with time."

See that? When things get confrontational Namgay does this martial arts thing with his mind. You know how in martial arts you use your opponent's strengths against him? In this case the opponent (that would be me) goes verbally charging at him and he either steps aside and acquiesces, he pleads guilty, or he grabs my arm as I'm charging and pulls me along so I run into the wall.

You'd think that I would be immune to this inattention to time having been married for so many years, that I would just chill and go with the flow. But no. It's my special hell. Or my ego, as he would say.

When he caves in and basically agrees to my argument, there is no argument. That caving in is not getting rid of ego. That's transcending ego. It is awesome. He knows if you pay attention to your feelings and just mark in a detached way when you're calm or not calm, angry, frustrated, elated, and if you can resist trying to control the feelings of others (which is what I do) and fighting with them or trying to manipulate them, that's transcending ego. You may still have the feelings brought on by ego. The feelings don't go away. You just acknowledge them. You don't try to change others because of them. It's as if you stand outside yourself. You rise above your need to be right.

When I'm at a loss for words I go to the place we all go when we need help, guidance, a way forward, inspiration, or great quotes to put on Facebook. I go to BrainyQuote.com. According to the site, the Buddha said, "In a controversy the instant we feel anger we have already ceased striving for the truth, and have begun striving for ourselves."

So we argue, I argue, because of the need to control things. Ego will always be there. What you want to do, and what he often does, is transcend the ego. Feel it, but don't act on it. Use it like that martial arts thing.

But just in case you think Namgay is not flappable, that he always maintains this Buddhist calm (a demeanor that, admittedly, he often has), it can be revealed that in fact, he's not always this way. Thank God.

We have a large collection of art books. Among them are 30 or so catalogs from Christie's and Sotheby's art auctions, going back years. These are gorgeous, full-color, fantastic tomes, and at night Namgay and I look through them and talk about the pictures. It's a great introduction for Namgay to Western art.

He has a hard time getting his head around the idea that a Mark Rothko canvas painted white with a small blob of red on the top and a slightly larger blob of red on the bottom, about six feet by four feet, can sell for $18–20 million. It makes him peevish. Once he was looking at a Sotheby's catalog and I heard him go "Ayyyyyy!" and then he threw the book across the room.

"What is it?!" I said. "You're not looking at Rothko again?"

He went to pick up the book and opened it to a minimalist painting that sold for $14 million. It was just a gray canvas. "That's whack," I said.

"I don't understand," he said, shaking his head. "This is nothing."

At times he must feel like he's been injected into some kind of alternate universe where nothing makes any sense. I know I do. Being a citizen of the world isn't for the fainthearted. Or for those with big egos.

But he has an edge because he has a Buddhist background, and so he understands a lot and has good coping skills. Ego when it's on display in Bhutan comes off as quite the spectacle because the normally quiet, unassuming Bhutanese don't act like we demonstrative, self-aggrandizing Westerners. Bhutanese most certainly have egos; they are just not so overtly out there with them.

One of the things Buddha taught after he attained enlightenment is the Four Noble Truths. I need to tell you about this because it's relevant and it's the Buddhist way to control ego and not get so caught up in the traps that make human beings kill, hate, destroy, hurt, and otherwise do nasty, destructive, and specifically self-destructive things.

Here are the Four Noble Truths as I see them.

1. Life is difficult. We can dance around this fact and we can have moments of happiness and bliss and we can enjoy some facets of our lives here on earth, but the sometimes crushingly depressing thing is that we're all going to die. But first we'll probably get old and sick. I'm sorry to be such a downer, but there it is.

2. Everything we do, and I mean everything,
    comes from trying to avoid the facts of the
    first Noble Truth. Our suffering in this world
    is a direct result of this desire—our wish to
    not struggle; to have great stuff; to be rich;
    to attain power, wealth, position; to order
    more shoes online. We suffer because of
    our wish to not die, and our wish for things
    that can't be. Our strong desire to overcome
    the fact that we're pretty insignificant in
    the scheme of things. Our hope that things
    outside of ourselves will fulfill us and we can
    pile everything up in front of the door to
    stave off death. All suffering comes from our
    struggle with the inevitable, and from our
    resistance to it. Ladies and gentlemen, may I
    present Ego.

3. Good news! You can get out of this cycle
    of desire and suffering. You really can,
    and the Buddha lays out an eightfold path
    that is, generally speaking, a blueprint for
    living a solid, straight-up life where you
    do enough for others around you and the
    focus of your actions is outside yourself so
    that you can see things as they are; have
    the right intent; speak, act, and work out of
    an ethical motivation; and make the proper
    effort and concentration. If we can do that,
    or degrees of that, we can ease our suffering.
    We abandon being led around by our egos,
    essentially.

4. Follow the path and be mindful, awake.
    See things as they really are. That's
    enlightenment.

Everyone wants to be happy. That's why we can some-times let our egos lead us. The road to happiness begins with that intent, that resolve to be happy. But happiness doesn't just happen. It's the result of action. That action may just be awareness, or a mindfulness, or a decision to do nothing, to just sit. Or it may be a choice between doing this or that. But you have to be conscious about it. You have to decide to be happy. Above all, to be happy you have to get the simple things right: eating, sleeping, breathing, walking, showing kindness to yourself and others, and all of the other ideas I describe in this book.

Before you do anything you have to calm down and find your center, that place inside of you that is your true self, the same no matter what is going on.

This is simple but seems complicated because the words and ideas are foreign to many of us. But this is a basic introduction, a drive-by. I'm not trying to recruit anyone, I'm just saying to check your ego and meditate on all the ways it trips you up. Almost anything difficult or problematic can be traced back to it.

To be responsive to the enormous changes we face in our lives, it's important to realize when we're being led by our egos and be aware of and respond to what's going on around us in a calm way. And then we can take action. To me, we just don't have enough time in our lives to do anything else.

WAKE UP

Looking out our living room window above Thimphu I know there's a town down there, but it's raining so I only see mountains in the clouds. It's double insulation. White clouds drape the tops of the mountains and give a canopy effect. It reminds me of when I was young and used bedsheets, blankets, and pillows to build forts with chairs and whatever else. The world couldn't come in, or so it seemed, perception being so much a part of reality. I like that feeling, the solitude and sense of peace and tranquility. It's hard to find in the world.

This is the magic of Bhutan. It's not a polluted place in any sense of the word. It is a refuge and a place to be restored. There is a healing quality to hiding out here and a feeling of being sequestered, protected. The mind quits racing. It's centering. Less "noise" going on around me allows more ideas to come in. It's not just me. Others have said so. It's good to find a sanctuary, a protected place with fewer obstacles to happiness, where we can find the strength and awareness to wake up.

For Buddhists, "waking up" is awareness, the precondition for enlightenment. Buddha is the awakened one. The word *Buddha* comes from *budhi*, which means "to wake up." If you're not Buddhist, waking up can mean paying a little more attention to the world around you and not being so absorbed in your own life, living in the present, fixating less on things that don't really matter, learning to be mindful, learning to see the world as it really is, being better and kinder, or understanding how your thoughts and actions affect everyone and everything. It's your call. I'm not trying to teach enlightenment. I'm interested in being awake.

"What do you like about the U.S.?" I ask Namgay. It's such an American question. A Bhutanese probably wouldn't ask. It's not part of their culture. But Namgay knows me and that's what I do, and part of the reason I ask is because his answers change, depending on his mood. His answers are barometers, reflections of his mood. I suppose the questions are barometers, too.

"What do I like? Walgreens," he says.

"What else?"

"I like that everything is so clean."

He's in that kind of mood.

"Do you think Americans have too much stuff?"

"No. Maybe."

"What do you think Americans could do to improve their lives?"

"I think Americans could wake up," he says.

Waking up is hard. I've been trying to do it my whole life.

I watch Namgay as he begins one of his thangkas by painting a thin mix of calcium chalk and gum onto cotton stretched and stitched inside a wooden frame. He rubs the cloth, pressing down hard with a smooth river rock, and repeats the process about four times, until the fabric is smooth and shiny and he can paint on it and the thangka can be rolled and unrolled for centuries without cracking the paint. It's about layering. And doing it until you get it right.

He draws the Buddha images and applies paint, starting always with the sky, then the earth background. He works inward, painting the Buddhas. The lesser ones (students or lamas) are painted first—their outer clothing, limbs, faces—so that the more important beings won't have to hang around waiting for the others to get finished. Each step is prescribed according to ancient traditions. The last thing painted is the Buddha's face, and the last thing on the face is the eyes. When he paints them (always early in the morning when the world is new and his hands are extra steady), the Buddha is said to "wake up."

He does this with every painting. I'm partial to the wrathful deities he paints. Legs splayed, they stand in yogic Warrior Pose for maximum leverage, the body center low, good for emerging, balance, or warding off attack. Their defining feature is that they are all engulfed in fire, their faces hideous, with multiple swollen, bulging eyes and fangs and often more than the requisite number of heads and limbs. They wear skull crowns indicating that they are Tantric, and gold-embossed robes or tiger skin loincloths and necklaces of severed heads and flayed bodies. I'm describing any number of deities like Dorje Drolo, the wrathful reincarnation of Padmasambhava; Vajrapani; and hundreds, maybe thousands more.

They wield flaming swords or arrows, or staffs, their hands and fingers frozen in various gestures, called *mudras*. There are 108 mudras. Think of praying hands, or a peace sign, or giving the finger. Mudras convey energy and are connected to yogic practices and various secret Tantric rituals, and they help with the flow of energy through the body. It's throwing up a gang sign, Tantric-style, and the metaphor is apt. But instead of drive-by shootings or rap careers, the wrathfuls are about protecting. These intimidating, complex, secret, ritualistic protectors have your back and can transmit to you your own salvation. They are your golden ticket, your fast track to enlightenment, and each has special skills. Three-eyed, red Dorje Drolo brandishes a dagger and a scorpion. He flew out of Tibet on the booty of his badass girlfriend, who changed herself into a tiger. Most, like the powerful protector Vajrapani, carry Tantric cattle prods called *dorjes* that squirt out electricity, or thunderbolts, or shocks of *vajra* (meaning light, lightning, indestructibility, precision, or enlightenment).

The wrathfuls might kick you in the face, but it's for your own good; they use their powers for good, and they might look and act frightening, but it is to shield you from danger and from your own idiocy while you sleep. They help you wake up, and they stand on disks or thrones littered with crushed human bodies. But don't get worked up about it. It's metaphor. The bodies represent attributes or habits in us that keep us from being enlightened: anger, greed, ignorance, all the things that blind us and make us do antithetical, unenlightened things. Although certain anger, it turns out, is a way to enlightenment. Isn't that interesting? The wrathfuls are mirrors that turn anger into wisdom. You may ask, *What's there to be so angry about?* You can't live in the world and not be angry. For most of us it's not the world we came in on and this is annoying—frightening, really. Or we feel paralyzed, pushed up into a corner or thwarted. So this "vajra" anger the wrathful deities exhibit is justified, necessary anger and very much a part of Buddhism. The wrathfuls are anger managers par excellence. Gaze upon them, meditate, control your anger, or your greed or whatever is your obstacle to enlightenment, and turn it back on itself.

I always thought Namgay's job, or calling, or karmic destiny, was to help wake people up. That's what he does with these thangkas he paints. The images of the pantheon of Buddhist deities are signs and symbols, road signs, to remind us to follow the path to enlightenment. Whatever your route—wisdom, compassion, sex, anger, stamp collecting, yoga (according to Tantric tradition anything can be used as a vehicle for enlightenment)— there is a deity or saint that personifies it. So in that sense, Namgay paints elaborate, exquisite wake-up calls. The front of this book is a painting by Namgay called *The Great Game*, which he painted when we were coming back to Bhutan from the U.S. I think with his rocket paintings Namgay is reminding himself to be mindful, to wake up. I know he thinks of himself in a rocket, going somewhere really fast, and with no idea where he's going. He says that's what he feels like in the U.S. His art is his way to explore and make sense of what's going on around him.

Anyone who tells you they are enlightened should be viewed suspiciously unless they are a Buddhist master from the Himalayas and have practiced their whole lives. But even then, if he or she is a truly enlightened being, he or she more than likely won't make that pronouncement and will encourage you to doubt. It's a long process and it's complicated, although in the Tantric school of

Buddhism in Bhutan, enlightenment could be as fast as the blink of an eye, the time it takes a traffic light to go from red to green.

The special brand of Buddhism in Bhutan and the rest of the Himalayas is a Tantric strain that says you can attain enlightenment in one lifetime. But it's a one-shot deal. If you don't find the right path and get to it, then you don't have any more chances.

Moving to Bhutan was my wake-up call, though even after all these years I am still trying to rouse myself. It made me strip everything away and build it back up again. I have been alone with my thoughts much of the time, which is useful for cultivating awareness and writing and daydreaming, but not so useful for other things. It confirmed for me that we have to get out of our own heads a lot of the time and do things for other people. But we all sort of know this already. We're all looking for effective ways to figure out what's important and what isn't. That's waking up.

Bhutanese pay attention to the rest of the world, but they also realize that Bhutan is unique, and they are also aware that the world can be a little envious and a little dangerous, too. Unless one lives here it's difficult to factor in just how profoundly isolation shapes the people—their outlook on the world and how they live. But in some ways they are the same as all of us. Talk with any young Bhutanese and the conversation eventually gets around to a desire to go to Australia or the U.S. and make some money to get some lumber to build a house.

"Why do you want a house?"

"To have some comfort, Madam."

"You'll have to work your ass off in Australia. And you might or might not make enough to send home and build a house."

"If we don't have money nothing can be done, *mo, Aney?*" (Isn't it, Aunty?) "No money, no Gross National Happiness."

Not long ago Kinlay and I took a trek up to a meditation center, Cheri Goempa, at the northern end of the Thimphu Valley. We drove about an hour to an ancient covered wooden bridge over a river where prayer flags fluttered over white rapids and crystal clear aquamarine water. The glacier-fed river formed a natural boundary for the Jigme Dorji Wangchuck National Park—acres of flora and accompanying forest creatures. About two kilometers away, up the mountain at Tango, monks have reported seeing Bengal tigers that have migrated away from the habitat encroachment and poachers of Northeast India for the sparse population and plentiful food of Bhutan. Former sea level dwellers, they have adapted to living above three thousand feet.

I thought about adaptation as we got out of the car and set off across the covered bridge and up the path for the lovely, albeit vigorous climb up the switchback trail to Cheri. My whole life has been about adaptation. We stopped halfway and had cheese, bread, and apples sitting at a *chorten,* a large Buddhist structure halfway between a statue and a mound that's built in a place of meditation, often on trails to temples. My old friend Dragana helped restore this one once so many years ago. It's beautiful and white and sort of dome shaped with a rectangular base. She was working in Bhutan for several years and used to complain because the contractor dumped sand and other supplies on the road beside the path up to the chorten and locals helped themselves to it. She could have restored four chortens with what she'd had to replace, she'd said.

On hearing this, her teacher, a lama, had made a clucking sound with his tongue, and said, "All the karma you gain by helping to restore the chorten will disappear in the blink of an eye with one negative word or thought." Then he laughed.

For all its seeming fluidity—finding your own path, letting it all unfold—pursuing the path to enlightenment seems actually quite rigorous. So much of life is about adapting and changing thoughts.

Cheri was built in 1619, by Shabdrung Ngawang Namgyal, the great unifier of Bhutan, who incidentally could turn himself into a raven and do things like make it rain snakes. He organized the Bhutanese to push back and eventually defeat the Tibetans, who had been invading from the north on and off for about two hundred years. Shabdrung was a high lama, artist, and political genius. He organized a dual religious and secular system of government, helped give Bhutan and the Bhutanese their distinctive cultural identity, and kept things progressing for many years. It's also true he came to Bhutan from Tibet because of a dispute about his legitimacy, so he was something of an immigrant, even a refugee, when he came here. But he adapted well.

The ancient buildings of Cheri, with many temples, perched on the side of a steep mountain, house about 40 monks. Small huts and lamaseries dot the mountainside above the main buildings, and this is where monks and lamas go to live and meditate in isolation—many for three years or more.

The hike took about an hour, so Kinlay and I went to sit on benches in the flagstone-floored courtyard where we could take in the money shot: a view of Thimphu Valley so beautiful as to be indescribable. The silence was as profound as the view. There was a good reason Shabdrung built here. I sat in silence myself, relishing the way a slight mist made it possible to see the air, and the fact that, out of all the places to end up in the world, I was lucky enough to end up here. Three monks came out of one of the temples to sit with us. We had come prepared to socialize, and shared almonds, plums, cheese, and biscuits. One of the monks brought us tea.

I'd met him before and we had a mutual friend, another monk named Sonam, who was friends with an American doctor who worked briefly in Bhutan. The doctor sent Sonam a plane ticket to come and be part of an American Buddhist community and now seven years later he was still in the U.S.

"Have you heard from Sonam?" I asked the monk.

"No."

I'd heard he was driving a taxi in New York and wondered if this was true.

"Yes. I believe he is working in New York," the monk said.

Here in Bhutan the highest aspiration one can have is to be a member of the clergy. A life as a monk (or nun) is a ticket to a higher birth in the next life, or possibly enlightenment—an end to the cycle of death and rebirth.

He and his friends, the monks of Cheri, were all in their 20s and early 30s and most had completed years of rigorous study. Training and religious studies aside, I couldn't help but wonder about the testosterone coursing through their veins, the wishes and desires and life force in them that would take a whole army of deities, wrathful and beatific, to turn into blissful, detached radiance.

In this fortress of solitude, this monastery on top of the world in this tiny country that is itself a stronghold, they had no access to the rest of the world, but they certainly had access to some kind of deep inner world. I wondered what they thought of Sonam. Was he some kind of folk hero—someone who was living the good life? His was a life they couldn't in their wildest dreams imagine, but I wondered what they did imagine. Bhutanese monks are supposed to be celibate and it was rumored that Sonam had taken a wife in the U.S.

"Would the door be open for him if he came back?" I asked. "Could he be a monk again?"

It would be difficult, the monks agreed. He'd have to do some petitioning, some purging—major tap dancing to the authorities. It wasn't out of the question but it wasn't usually done.

We all knew he probably wouldn't come back.

I couldn't let it go. "In his next life, after he'd been a monk, will he have a bad reincarnation?" The cosmos doesn't deal kindly with defectors.

Yes, all the monks agreed he'd have a low birth. He'd lose major karmic points. He was on the fast track to enlightenment and he gave it up.

I get all bristly when Westerners who visit Bhutan think there shouldn't be any Westernization, that Bhutan and the Bhutanese shouldn't change or watch so much television, that it is Buddhist Disney World or a museum. Namgay feels it, too. Once he said about a group of American Buddhists, "I think they think my farts smell like incense." Some of them like to wear Buddhist robes and walk around. This vexes some of our monk friends who wear the robes as a symbol of their vows to renounce the world.

I always say Bhutan isn't a museum. It changes. Why should it be held to a higher standard? But it's not that simple. I'm lucky to have come from the U.S., and unless something crazy happens I can come and go. It's easy for me to say, but from my perspective, Bhutanese lives are so much better and they should all stay put. Of course I don't say that to the monks. I say something about how I hope Sonam is having a good life and how complicated it all is.

"It's okay," the monk says. "It's just karma."

This is what I'm thinking, too. I think it's a good thing to live as if all that we do—good things, bad things, indifferent things—gets tallied up on a cosmic score-board. If we can bring a lot of kindness and compassion to the world and do good works, then we'll stockpile some good karma. Whether or not karma is real doesn't matter. It's a moot point. Live as if it's true. Live believing that your actions accrue consequences, either good or bad.

On the way down the mountain I'm still thinking about Sonam in New York City. It's the middle of the night there and maybe he's driving somewhere with city lights all around him, and the pavement is glistening because it's rained. In some ways I'm sad for him because he's not here in this beautiful place living up to his birthright. But I don't know Buddhist doctrine and I know it's a tricky subject. I also know he's had some outstanding training and secret instruction about how to live in cloistered devotion in the mountains in Bhutan, and how to work toward enlightenment. Perhaps this study and instruction gives him some insights to wake up, or at the very least to overcome the surfeit of rage manifesting on the streets of New York, and to work against fear and despair, and to cultivate a compassionate heart. Wherever he is, he's probably good to have around. He ought to be able to manifest some clarity.

Sometimes I get so confused and I can't follow the thread, and I think my brain will explode with too much information. The truth is I'm not always kind. Like everybody else, sometimes I fall into a critical view of myself and the world. I teeter on despair, and occasionally succumb to it. Sometimes I'm not a very good parent. I work too hard. I don't work hard enough. It's possible I've done unspeakably horrible things. Remember, I woke up with donut filling in my hair.

Not many of us are fully living up to our birthright as stewards of the earth, as beings capable of manifesting compassion and kindness. Our minds do us in as well as the obstacles, real or imagined, we face every day.

All this occurs to me as I'm coming down the mountain, but then I tell myself to breathe. And in that breathing I can manifest gratitude. I am grateful for the air that flows into my body and keeps me alive. I thank the universe. I can enjoy the walk. That's happiness.

I know that I'll go home and we'll cook some dinner and hang out and later I'll get into bed. I might sleep soundly and have wonderful dreams, and wake up with the sun to a new day. Or I might be wakeful, for whatever reason, and toss in the bed or stare out into the darkness. But even if I can't sleep so well, I'm going to get up in the morning anyway. And even if my head hurts and my eyes sting from lack of sleep, I'm going to give myself a free pass. In that moment of wakefulness, I'm cleaning the slate. I'm going to start again and try to get it right.

I know if I do this enough, I will wake up.

ACKNOWLEDGMENTS

I am lucky in my life to be something of a magnet for buddhas, bodhisattvas, and protectors. Sometimes they might give a lesson, or a gentle nudge, or even shoot fire in my direction.

I want to thank Joe and Judy Barker, who gave me support, beautiful views, many laughs, much encouragement, and most of all: big dreams. They are extraordinary people, beyond generous with their time and resources, and I am so lucky to know them and I love them both very much.

I especially want to thank John McQuiston for pointing me to his elegant, simple, and illuminating book, *Always We Begin Again*. It's not hyperbole to say it changed my life. Who knew? Also thanks to Robbie for the lovely day in Paro and the pizza and beer.

Thanks to Laurie Abkemeier, physically a very tiny, elegant woman, but a powerhouse of a human and the best friend a writer can have. I don't know how people write books without her. I'm sure it's possible, but I can't believe it's as much fun.

Thanks to the exceptional Hay House team: Patty Gift, the extraordinary acquisitions editor who is beautiful inside and out, Sally Mason, Alexandra Gruebler, Monica Meehan, Christy Salinas, cover designer Nita Ybarra, and especially Reid Tracy and the remarkable

Louise Hay, who started it all. They all make me better. I am forever grateful.

There are so many people who helped me while I was writing this, in Bhutan and in the U.S., and I can't thank them all here, but I want to mention Lonnie Frey, who read a draft of this manuscript and was very encouraging and who is pure joy to spend time with and who makes me laugh a lot. Thanks to Will Frey for showing me a Bhutan I've never seen in his remarkable photos.

To Marie Brown, Lynee Durham, Marcus Leong, Thinley Dorji (always), John Halpin, Louise Dorji, Ariana Maki, Pem Tandi, and Tim Towers, a big thank you. You may or may not know how much you helped me and that you are in my heart, so I'm putting it out there. You were all at various times encouraging and inspiring. I'm grateful to know you. You make me happy.

I want to give special thanks to my father, Perry Leaming, for giving me the gene that likes change and for being a great pilot.

A big thank you and love to Phurba Namgay for letting me write about him in a revelatory way.

Thank you to everyone at Pitcher Spring Farm. Also, huge thanks to Holly Quick, whose name is a full sentence and who is on familiar terms with the bluebirds of happiness.

ABOUT THE AUTHOR

Linda Leaming is a writer whose work has appeared in *Ladies' Home Journal, Mandala, The Guardian U.K., A Woman's Asia: True Stories* (Travelers' Tales, 2005)*,* and many other publications. Eric Weiner included her in his 2008 bestseller, *The Geography of Bliss*. She has an MFA in fiction from the University of Arizona, and she regularly speaks about Bhutan at colleges, churches, seminars and book groups.

www.lindaleaming.com
www.twitter.com/lindaleaming

NOTES

NOTES

NOTES

NOTES

Hay House Titles of Related Interest

YOU CAN HEAL YOUR LIFE, the movie, starring Louise Hay & Friends
(available as a 1-DVD programme and an expanded 2-DVD set)
Watch the trailer at: www.LouiseHayMovie.com

THE SHIFT, the movie, starring Dr. Wayne W. Dyer
(available as a 1-DVD programme and an expanded 2-DVD set)
Watch the trailer at: www.DyerMovie.com

BE HAPPY: Release the Power of Happiness in YOU,
by Robert Holden PhD

HOW TO STAY SANE IN A CRAZY WORLD, by Sophia Stuart

*SECRETS OF MEDITATION: A Practical Guide to Inner Peace
and Personal Transformation,* by davidji

WALKING HOME: A Pilgrimage from Humbled to Healed,
by Sonia Choquette

All of the above are available at your local bookstore,
or may be ordered by contacting Hay House (see next page).

We hope you enjoyed this Hay House book. If you'd like to receive our online catalogue featuring additional information on Hay House books and products, or if you'd like to find out more about the Hay Foundation, please contact:

Hay House UK, Ltd., Astley House, 33 Notting Hill Gate, London W11 3JQ
Phone: 0-20-3675-2450 • *Fax:* 0-20-3675-2451
www.hayhouse.co.uk • www.hayfoundation.org

Published and distributed in the United States by: Hay House, Inc., P.O. Box 5100, Carlsbad, CA 92018-5100
Phone: (760) 431-7695 or (800) 654-5126
Fax: (760) 431-6948 or (800) 650-5115
www.hayhouse.com®

Published and distributed in Australia by: Hay House Australia Pty. Ltd., 18/36 Ralph St., Alexandria NSW 2015 • *Phone:* 612-9669-4299 *Fax:* 612-9669-4144 • www.hayhouse.com.au

Published and distributed in the Republic of South Africa by: Hay House SA (Pty), Ltd., P.O. Box 990, Witkoppen 2068
Phone/Fax: 27-11-467-8904 • www.hayhouse.co.za

Published in India by: Hay House Publishers India, Muskaan Complex, Plot No. 3, B-2, Vasant Kunj, New Delhi 110 070 • *Phone:* 91-11-4176-1620 • *Fax:* 91-11-4176-1630 • www.hayhouse.co.in

Distributed in Canada by: Raincoast Books, 2440 Viking Way, Richmond, B.C. V6V 1N2 • *Phone:* 1-800-663-5714
Fax: 1-800-565-3770 • www.raincoast.com

Take Your Soul on a Vacation

Visit www.HealYourLife.com® to regroup, recharge, and reconnect with your own magnificence. Featuring blogs, mind-body-spirit news, and life-changing wisdom from Louise Hay and friends.

Visit www.HealYourLife.com today!